BUFFALO
BROADCASTING
VOLUME ONE: 1920-1970

Steve Cichon

buffalostories.com

ISBN 978-0-9828739-3-9

Published by Buffalo Stories LLC and staffannouncer.com

Contents

On the covers   5
On a personal note   8
Setting the record straight- Radio's birth in Buffalo 11

1920s
The earliest days of Buffalo broadcasting   16

1930s
Buffalo & The Lone Ranger   45
Stoopnagle & Budd   49
Roger Baker   51
WBEN – The Buffalo Evening News Station   56
Roy Albertson's WBNY   62
FDR in Buffalo as President   64
Father Justyn's Rosary Hour   70

1940s
Stations on the move   76
Buffalo's first look at TV   79
Buffalo's radio staff musicians   80
Buffalo morning radio wars, 1940s style   95
Buffalo radio at war   103
WBEN-TV signs on, 1948   112
AHK   126
The Buffalo Bills of the AAFC, 1946-49   131
Bennett High's future star power, 1946   133
Billy and Reggie Keaton   141
The WGR Flashcast   143
Ralph Hubbell   145

1950s
In 1950,   149
Wrestling from Memorial Auditorium   150
Early 50s radio   155
Husband & Wife teams   169
Brought to you by...   184
Buffalo's forgotten TV pioneers: WBES & WBUF   187

Buffalo's Willis Conover	193
The Rico Family	199
Buffalo's Polka King	203
Buffalo's last staff organist	204
For the kiddos on Ch.4	207
Beginnings of a teenage revolution:	
The Hound, Lucky Pierre, & Hernando	217
Legacy of the Seneca-Babcock Boys Club	223
"The calm before the storm"	228
WGR-TV, Buffalo's Ch.2	237
Guy King ushers in bad boy rock 'n' roll	249
Dick Lawrence brings Top-40 to Buffalo	253
Western Connections	268
Jack Sharpe and WEBR's Trafficopter	270
Buffalo's third and final VHF: WKBW-TV, Ch.7	272
The relegated role of women, (con't.)	281
Public Broadcasting comes to Buffalo	286
1960s	
Boost Buffalo, It's Good for You!	305
WBEN AM-FM-TV's new home, 1960	307
A new voice for Buffalo's Black community, WUFO	311
The Sound of the City, WEBR	320
One of America's Two Great Radio Stations: WKBW	322
More listeners start tuning to FM	343
Irv, Rick, & Tom	355
Cable TV comes to WNY	364
Rocketship 7 & Commander Tom	366
Beatlemania hits WKBW	377
Ramblin' Lou & The Family Band	384
Dialing for Dollars	387
Ground up by radio: Bill Masters & Frank Benny	406
On the radio, on the telephone: John Otto	415
Jeff Kaye & KB's War of the Worlds	423
Sandy Beach begins a 52-year Buffalo run	425
Thanks....	429
Steve Cichon	430

On the covers

The collage of 270 photos on the front and back covers come together to tell the history of Buffalo Broadcasting before you even open the book. This is a brief description of each photo, row by row.

Front Cover:

Front cover, row 1: Van Miller at the Buffalo Braves mic; Eyewitness News crew; Susan Banks, Ch. 7; Carol Jasen, Ch.4; Jim Santella at WYSL-FM; Ed Little, WBEN; Howard Simon, WBEN; Promo the Robot, Rocketship 7; Susan King, WGR-TV, Stan Barron, WBEN

Front cover, row 2: Roger Baker, WGR; Santa with Forgetful & Grumbles the elves, Ch. 4; Henry Marcotte, June Bacon-Bercey, WGR-TV; Jack Mahl, Atlantic Weatherman, Ch.2; Mark Leitner, WBEN News; Stoopnagle & Budd, WMAK; Brian Blessing & Mike Robitaille, Hockey Hotline, Empire Sports Network; Al Vaughters, Ch.4; Mary Travers, Ch.7; Taylor & Moore, WPHD; Chuck Healy, Ch.4

Front cover, row 3: Kevin O'Connell, WBEN-TV; Art Wander, WGR; John DiSciullo, WKBW; Bill and Mildred Miller, WBEN-TV; Nolan Johannes, Dialing for Dollars; Carol Jasen, Ch.4; John Zach & Susan Rose, WBEN; Howdy Doody & Buffalo Bob Smith; Tom Connolly, WBEN; Adam Keefe, Ch.7; WGR-TV bumper.

Front cover, row 4: Ron Hunter, Ch.2; Stan Roberts, WGR; Sandy White, Ch.4; Tim Fleischer, Ch.7.

Front cover, row 5: Charles R. Turner Heating & Cooling; Jacquie Walker, Ch.4; Greg Bauch, WGR; Cindy DiBiasi, Ch.7

Front cover, row 6: Ted Darling, Voice of the Sabres; Anne Simon, Ch.7; Doris Jones, Ch.2; Al Wallack Jazz in the Nighttime

Front cover, row 7: Buffalo Bob Smith & Mike Randall, Ch.7; Jon Summers & Dan Neaverth, WKBW; Larry Sales, Ch.7; Commander Tom, Ch.7; Marty Biniasz; Irv Weinstein, Ch.7; Clint Buehlman, WBEN; Danny Neaverth, Bells; Elvis Presley and George "Hound Dog" Lorenz; WBNY cruiser; Jay Moran, WNSA.

Front cover, row 8: Rich Newberg, Ch.4; Barry Lillis, Barry's Cat's Pajamas, Ch.2; Sheila Murphy, Ch.2; Don Postles Ch.7; John Otto, WGR; Ramblin' Lou Schriver, WWOL; Brandy Scrufari & Zig Fracassi, WJJL; Bill Devine & Goldie Gardner, WNED; AM Buffalo; Sandy Beach, WKBW; John Corbett, Ch.4

Front cover, row 9: Jack Mindy, WBEN; Kevin Jolly, YNN, Paul Woodson, Ch.4, Dooley O'Rourke, Ch.2, Mark Leitner, WNED, George Richert, Ch.4, Claudine Ewing, Ch.2; Bill Lacy, WBEN; Fun? Wow!, Fantasy Island commercial; Art "Mr. Food" Ginsburg; Al Anscombe, WKBW; Don "Keller" Yearke, Ch.7; Tom McCrea, John Zach, Tom Shannon, Dan Neaverth; Les Trent, Ch.2; Ted Shredd & Tom Ragan, WEDG; WBEN and WEBR, The News Stations, 1941

Front cover, row 10: Jeff Kaye & Rod Roddy, WKBW Radio; John Corbett, Chuck Lampkin, Van Miller, Ch.4 news; Danny Moves my Fanny patch, Joey from Super Duper; Art Wander, Bob Koshinski, Larry Felser, Ed Kilgore, Pros & Cons Empire Sports Network; Rich Kellman & Sheila Murphy, Ch.2; Johnny & Jimmy, the Dialing for Dollars Band; Kevin O'Connell, Disco-Step-By-Step; Don Polec, Ch.7; Jacquie Walker & Chuck Gurney, Ch.4; Dick Rifenburg, Ch.4

100 Years of Buffalo Broadcasting

Front cover, row 11: Carl Russo, Medaille College; Pete Weber & John Murphy, WBEN; Jimmy Lyons, WUFO; Roger Lund, Ch.7; WWOL deejay; Mylous Hairston, Ch.4; WBEN-TV cameras in 1948; Bob Koshinski, Ch.7; Van Miller, Voice of the Bills; Joe Schlaerth & Mike Mombrea, Ch.4; Clip Smith Ch.7

Front cover, row 12: Beat the Champ open, Ch.4; Brad Riter, WGR; Larry Norton, 97 Rock; Elliot Shapiro, Gary Deeb, Doug Smith, Buffalo Evening News; Kevin Keenan, Brandy Scrufari, Ed Little, Bill Lacy, WBEN; Dave Thomas, Ch.7; Milt Ellis, Voice of the Aud & WDCX; Van Miller, Bob Koop, Lou McNally, Ch.4; Val Townsend, WEDG; NewsCenter 2 open; Bill & Reggie Keaton, WGR

Front cover, row 13: Carl Koch & The WBEN Trio; Al Wallack, WEBR; Buffalo Braves logo; WKBW News license plate; Jay Fredericks (Fritz Coleman), WBEN; Mayor Masiello with WNUC t-shirt; Tom Bauerle, WGR; Willy WNIA; Craig Matthews, WHTT; Clinton Buehlman, WGR; Henry Brach and Danny Neaverth, WKBW

Front cover, row 14: Virgil Booth, Ch.4; Danny Neaverth, Tom Shannon, Rod Roddy, WKBW; Eyewitness news open; John Lascalles and David Cheskin at Rendez-Vous, WGR

Front cover, row 15: Fr. Justyn Figas of The Rosary Hour; Chuck Lampkin, Ch.4; George "Hound Dog" Lorenz; Keith Radford and Kathleen Leighton, Ch.7; Pete Anderson, Q-102; Van Miller & Stan Barron; Tom Jolls, Ch.7; Howard Simon, WBEN; Duke Ellington with Liz Dribben, Ch.7; Shane Brother Shane Gibson, WGR; Mary Alice Demler, Ch.2

Front cover, row 16: Randy Bushover, WBEN; Laurie Short, Ch.4; Ralph Hubbell, WBEN; Frank Benny, WGR; Jim Santella, WGR-FM; Jeff Kaye, WBEN; Brian Kahle & Linda Pellegrino, Ch.7; Danny Neaverth, Oldies 104; Mike Robitaille, Jim Lorenz, Rick Jeanneret, Ted Darling at the Aud; Jack Armstrong, WKBW

Front cover, row 17: Billy Fuccillo, Kathy Ansuini, Ch.7; Trish Mattimore, WKBW; Tom Langmyer, WBEN; Maria Genero, Ch.4; Van Miller, WBEN; Gov. Rockefeller and Paula Drew; John Murphy, Ch.7; WKBW record album; Chuck Healy, Ch.4; John Beard, Carol Crissey, Ch.4

Back Cover:

Back cover, row 1: Brian Kahle, Nancy Foreman, Ch.7; Tim Wenger & Susan Rose, WBEN; Victoria Hong, Ch.2; Mike Randall, Bob Stilson, Promo the Robot, Commander Tom, Ch.7; Clint Buehlman, WBEN; Jim Taylor, Ted Hackett, Tom Shannon, Don Keller, Dick Braun, Gene Nelson, WKBW; Don Paul, Ch.4; Gary McNamara, WBEN; Tom Jolls, Ch.7; Ch.17's Great TV Auction and the Quickies Board; Rich Kellman and Don Postles, Ch.2

Back cover, row 2: Eyewitness Newsreel; Bob Wells, WEBR

Back cover, row 3: Sally Work, WBEN; Ch.2 logo

Back cover, row 4: Dave Gillen, Q-102; Don Moffit, Debbie Stamp, PM Magazine; John Murphy, WBEN; Ken Philips, Ch.4; Ron Dobson, WBEN; Irv Weinstein, Ch.7; Bill Lacy, Kevin Keenan, WBEN; Dave Thomas, Johnny Banaszak, Nolan Johannes, Jimmy Edwin, Dialing for Dollars, Ch.7; Danny Neaverth, WKBW; Rick Jeanneret, Ted Darling, Mike Robitaille, Jim Lorenz; John Pauly, Ch.7

Back cover, row 5: Jack Eno, WEBR; Tommy Shannon, WKBW; Liberace, Mildred Miller, Bill Miller—Meet the Millers; Art Wander; Jack Kemp, Van Miller; Jacquie Walker, Bob Koop, Carol Jasen, Ch.4; Fred Klestine, WKBW; Chuck Healy, Beat the Champ, Ch.4; Tom Whalen, WBEN; Ch.2 mic flag, mid 80s; Dave Brubeck and Liz Dribben, Ch.7

Back cover, row 6: Rick Azar, Ch.7; Stan Jasinski; Dog & Polly Smith, Ch.4; Tom Jolls, Ch.7; Ramblin' Lou Schriver and the Family Band; Ch.7 Live Eye

Back cover, row 7: WWOL, Shelton Square; Andrew Siff, Ch.7; Steve Cichon, WBEN; Les Trent, Ch.2; Barry Lillis, WJJL; Bill Mazer, WKBW

Back cover, row 8: Stan Roberts for Mister Donut, WBUF; Al Meltzer, Bills Play-by-play, WKBW; Danny McBride and Ed Tucholka; John Jarrett, WJJL; Frank Wojnarski's Pic-A-Polka Band, Ch.2; Nan Cooper, WBEN

Back cover, row 9: Ed Little, WBEN; WGR-TV's elves; Irv Weinstein, Ch.7; Tony Battilana, Ch.4; WKBW Radio studios, 1430 Main Street; Jim Kelley & Howard Simon, WBEN

Back cover, row 10: Mark Leitner, WBEN; John Beard, Ch.4; Jeff Kaye, WKBW; Keith Luke, WYSL; Helen Neville, WGR; The Jolly Little Baker, Kaufman's Rye Bread

Back cover, row 11: WIVB-TV Sign, Elmwood Ave; Rod Roddy, The Price is Right; Tony Smith, WUFO; John Demerle, Empire Sports Network; Hank Nevins, WBEN; Irv, Ch.7; WBEN-TV test pattern; Janet Snyder, Kiss 98.5; Marty Gleason, WBEN; Rick Pfeiffer, Ch.4; Doris Jones, Ch.2

Back cover, row 12: Captain Mike Mearian and Buttons the Cabin Boy, Ch.4; Joey Reynolds, WKBW; Brian Kahle, Ch.7; Jungle Jay Nelson, WKBW; Rick Jeanneret, Voice of the Sabres; John Otto, WGR; Van Miller, WBEN; WGR mobile Studio; Irv Weinstein, Don Postles, Ch.7; Uncle Jerry Brick, Ch.4; John Zach, Steve Cichon, WBEN

Back cover, row 13: George Lorenz, The Ol'Hound Dog, PM Magazine still, Mr. Whatnot Jack Paupst, Ch.17; Tom Kelly, WBEN; Ken Philips, Gene Kelly, Al Fox, Jack Ogilvie, John Luther, WBEN; Ernie Warlick, Ch.2; Foster Brooks, WGR; Richard Reeve, Ch.4; Sandy Beach, Don Berns, Jack Armstrong, Casey Piotrowski, Jack Sheridan, Dan Neaverth, Bob McRae, WKBW; WBEN-TV cameras at the Aud; Larry Sales, Ch.7

Back cover, row 14: Lucky Pierre, WBNY; Roger Christian, WBEN-FM; Esther Huff and Clint Buehlman at Hengerer's, WBEN; Rich Kellman & Molly McCoy, Ch.2; Dan Neaverth, WKBW; Wadi Sawabini, Ch.4; Ward Fenton, Ch.4; Jon & Howard Simon, WNSA; Rufus Coyote, WYSL; Rick Maloney, WNSA; Barry Lillis Ch.2

Buffalo Broadcasters Hall of Fame ceremony group photo, 1998. Marty Biniasz, Phil Beuth, Bob Smith, Ed Little, Jack Horohoe, Jack McLean, Al Wallack, Leia Militello, Rick Azar, Irv Weinstein, Carol Jasen, Lee Coppola, Iney Wallens, Tom Jolls, Steve Cichon, Simon Goldman, Gary Deeb, Van Miller, Steve Mitchell, Mike Igoe, JR Reid, Don Yearke.

On a personal note...

While organizing some of my archives very early in the COVID quarantine, it became clear that there was a book about the history of Buffalo broadcasting screaming out from the piles of material.

Well, that's partly true. I've really been writing this book since I was about 6 years old.

Of course, I didn't realize it then, but that's when we'd visit Grandpa Coyle, and he was transfixed by the small black, paint-splattered radio sitting next to his orange rocking chair in the living room.

The exciting voices of Van Miller and Ted Darling came out of that little radio when Gramps, who was a season ticket holder for the Bills and the Sabres, would listen to away games. He'd throw his arms in the air and mumble a lot, and ask me to go get him another stubby bottle of Schmidt's or Labatt 50 out of the fridge.

A few blocks away, Grandpa Cichon would sit on his porch with a similar radio, but a different experience. Instead of winding him up, Stan Jasinski's polka program seemed to make life slow down into a warm smile for Gramps.

"What is he saying?" we'd ask my first-generation American grandfather, as Jasinski spoke in Polish. He'd make up something silly, but we couldn't be quite sure whether what he was saying was true, because who else knew Polish?

Back at our home, the best bonding time with my ol'man came when we'd sit for an hour and watch the news together. I became acquainted with Rich Kellman and John Beard and Irv Weinstein as I learned numbers on that round, loud, clunking TV dial--when I'd act as Dad's channel-changer in the days before we had a remote.

A few years later, my friend's dad took our Cub Scout troop to the radio station where he worked—and my face just about fell off. I was hooked. I started waking up at 5am on Saturdays to go to work with him. That friend had a radio station set up in his basement where we'd make tapes.

When we moved, I had a "radio station" in my house. I'd make tapes and call talk shows. I recorded and saved my call to a disc jockey making a birthday request for my brother doing a really terrible Ronald Reagan impression. I was 10 years old.

At 15, I wrote letters to every radio station in Western New York, asking if they needed an intern. The only one to respond was the boss at my favorite station-- Kevin Keenan at WBEN. I spent every moment of that summer at the station, and at the end of summer fulfilled a dream and went on the payroll as a weekend board operator. I was a high school junior working in radio, having the most fun of my life and feeling fantastic.

One of my first moments understanding that I was holding the power of radio in my own hands came with news of Ted Darling's shocking death from Pick's disease at the age of only 61.

Only 18 myself at the time, I wasn't a huge hockey fan-- but I had grown up loving the sound, the feel, the excitement, *the magic* of Ted Darling. I also felt the sadness of listeners who filled the airwaves remembering the great broadcaster and lamenting the loss of this great icon.

By then a full-fledged producer, I internalized the passion and grief around me, and put it into my work, spending hours combing through and editing highlights of his play-by-play to create a Ted Darling tribute which aired on WBEN.

The heartfelt and overwhelming reaction to that piece changed me and changed the way I looked at my job. To that point, I knew I could use radio to be goofy and have fun, but in that moment, I learned that radio could be an outlet for me, personally, to create things that are meaningful to people by reflecting what they long for and how they feel in my work.

Everything I've done in radio, TV, and print since then—including this book—has been a manifestation of that powerful realization.

It was one of thousands of lessons I learned by doing, working alongside many of the greatest broadcasters in Buffalo's history. You know some of the names— folks like Van Miller and Danny Neaverth, but just as importantly are some of the folks you'll get to know as you read this book and its future companion volumes-- the folks who'd run 2,000 feet of cable for a live shot or who pressed the button to start the commercial when Van stopped talking.

Not everyone grew up working in radio and TV like I did, but it's almost impossible to have lived over the last century without having the people of radio and TV become part of your family and part of the fabric of who you are.

They have been with you during the great and the dark moments in history and there for happiness and sadness in your life.

They are the broadcasters who whispered out of the transistor radios under our pillows, filled the screens in our living rooms, blared out the speakers in our car, and these days-- stream on our phones and tablets.

It still feels like a dream to me that I have had the opportunity to be a part of your life in that way over the course of 25 years… especially knowing what the people I've listened to and watched have meant to me.

I mean all this to say that the book feels as much like a family tree as it does a book about Buffalo Broadcasting.

With that mindset, I didn't want to leave anything out. As I began work on the actual layout of the book, it was clear that there was just too much for a single volume, so I split the hundred years in half… and here we are.

By the time you read this, know that I've already began squirreling away the photos and stories that will make up a history of the last 50 years of broadcasting—and it will be a much more complete work with your stories and photos contributed. You can start that ball rolling with an email to **steve@buffalostories.com**.

May your joy in reading this book be the same that mine has been in spending a lifetime putting it together—smiling, enjoying, and remembering the people who've added color, vibrance, and a sense of community to our Western New York lives for a century.

Steve Cichon
June, 2020

Setting the record straight- Radio's birth in Buffalo

In history, definitives can be hard. Publicists are often most loose with noting something as "first" or "tallest" or "oldest," because it sounds better than "one of the first," one of the tallest," or "one of the oldest." A good publicist knows that even if you can't be 100% sure of your claim-- so long as no one is quick to challenge it, and so long as it gets repeated often enough, it becomes "fact."

There were decades of advancements that lead up to the day that most historians agree was the birthdate of modern radio-- November 2, 1920.

That's when Experimental station 8XK in Pittsburgh--which would eventually become KDKA--broadcast the results of the Presidential Election in what is often heralded as "the start of the radio era."

But Pittsburgh was not alone on the radio dial that night. That same historic night, at the same exact time, election results broadcast by The Buffalo Evening News also came in loud and clear on wireless sets across Western New York.

Radio listeners in Buffalo and Pittsburgh had the same mind-blowing, history-making experience on what was a rainy evening in Western New York. People sat around their wireless sets in their living rooms, finding out in real time that Warren G. Harding had been elected President.

The newly born power of radio was equally evident in both cities, and the marvel and wonder surrounding this growing technology was exactly the same. In fact, it was all part of the same plan.

The American Radio Relay League, an amateur radio operator group still in business to this day, created a plan to "beat the regular wire service in getting the election returns to the public."

"The plan is to have a good amateur transmitting station in each important city throughout the country send broadcast via radio the available data in his territory once every hour. This information will be picked up by thousands of radio amateurs who will arrange, through the local

11

newspapers or in some other manner, to bulletin the returns for the general public in their respective territories."

All this is described in a Pittsburgh Daily Post article, which goes on to say that Frank Conrad's 8XK will take part in the effort for Pittsburgh area listeners.

AMATEUR WIRELESS OPERATORS TO TRY BROADCAST SCHEME AT ELECTION TIME

A scheme wherein the amateur wireless operators of the country will endeavor to beat the regular wire service in getting the presidential election returns to the public is being worked out by the American Radio Relay League, a National organization of amateur radio enthusiasts.

The plan is to have a good amateur transmitting station in each important city throughout the country send broadcast via radio the available data in his territory, once every hour, on a five-minute schedule. This information will be picked up by many thousands of radio amateurs who will arrange, through the local newspapers or in some other manner, to bulletin the returns for the general public in their respective territories.

The operator of the radio station assigned in each city will enlist the services of a few local men to assist in collecting the data by having them stationed at the headquarters of the two political factions in his city, or at the offices of local newspapers, where reliable first hand returns from that territory can be obtained at the earliest moment. These assistants will phone the information to the transmitting station in good time to broadcast on the schedule arranged. The remainder of the hour is devoted to picking up returns from other territories being trans-

mitted by radio stations performing the same service in other cities, these returns to be given publication on local bulletins.

In Pittsburgh, Frank P. Conrad of Wilkinsburg, known to radio amateurs as Radio 8XK, has been selected by the league to broadcast the returns from this territory. The Radio Engineering Society of Pittsburgh, Inc., an organization affiliated with the American Radio Relay League, plans to furnish free bulletin service at their headquarters, 431 Sixth avenue, throwing the returns received from other territories by wireless on a screen in front of its headquarters. C. E. Urban has been appointed to take charge of this service.

Profiteering Case Quashed by Court

Violation of Constitutional Rights Held.

For the first time in Federal district court here indictments secured against

Pittsburgh Daily Post, October 21, 1920

A Buffalo Evening News article announcing the broadcast of election returns for Western New York doesn't mention the larger plan, but does offer more detail about the Buffalo plan.

"Evening News" Will Spread Election Story by Wireless

Newspaper Has Arranged With Charles C. Klinck Jr., to Broadcast Results Obtained From Its Seven Agencies

Wireless will be included in the election return service given by the EVENING NEWS this year. Arrangements have just been made with Charles C. Klinck Jr. to broadcast results by wireless telephone from his home at 35 West Parade avenue.

These returns may be picked up by anyone with a receiving set within a radius of 75 miles or more, dependent on weather conditions. Klinck will begin sending out returns at 6 o'clock and will continue to give the service until 11.

City returns will be supplied him from the EVENING NEWS office as soon as they are received, also state and national returns. The NEWS will be able to give a very complete report, with seven agencies supplying the service.

Klinck is electrical instructor at Technical High school. He has one of the best wireless outfits in this section of the country.

Buffalo Evening News, October 28, 1920

So how is it that high school text books say Pittsburgh's broadcast that night was "the historic first commercial broadcast" but the remarkably similar experience that listeners had in Western New York (and in other cities around the country) at the very same time goes unmentioned?

The simple answer is—the amateur operator in Pittsburgh, Frank Conrad, worked for Westinghouse Electric. Westinghouse had a lot riding on getting its radio equipment and vacuum tubes out on the market before David Sarnoff's Radio Corporation of America did.

Westinghouse saw gold in making sure that when people bought radios—they had something reliable to listen to. The company also saw an edge in being able to promote that they'd got a head start over RCA.

Westinghouse's Pittsburgh station, the one that would eventually take the call letters KDKA, was first to broadcast in the battle between Westinghouse and RCA. *That* was the original claim. Even the Pittsburgh newspaper makes it clear that the station was one of many—tied for first, if we mark that day as the start of the modern era of radio.

As it often happens, Westinghouse's heavy marketing very quickly dropped the "tied for first" notion, and over the last century, history has accepted the muddled marketing of a radio manufacturer as fact.

Meanwhile, in Buffalo, nobody was bending the truth of radio's birth to sell vacuum tubes. In fact, the historic events that took place that rainy night were mostly lost as history quietly turned the page. The high school electronics teacher who broadcast Buffalo's first elections results didn't work for a giant corporation.

In fact, after participating in the world's first scheduled radio broadcast, Charles Klinck continued a normal life as an electronics teacher for the next four decades at various Buffalo high schools and then at Buffalo State Teachers College (Buff State) and Erie County Technical Institute (ECC). For Klinck, that night was about nothing more than using technology to get Western New Yorkers the news faster.

The point is, the listener experience was the same in Buffalo and in Pittsburgh. Thirty years later, teens who were choosing between WKBW and WNIA for their rock 'n' roll didn't care that KB was in a million-dollar broadcast center and WNIA was (and is) in a ranch house in Cheektowaga. From its infancy, radio has been the theater of the mind.

Before the 1920s were out, Westinghouse and KDKA mounted bronze plaques and created marketing pieces calling their broadcast "the world's first scheduled broadcast." Buffalo's participation that night was so utterly forgotten that the Courier-Express didn't even mention any connection to radio when Klinck—Buffalo's first broadcaster-- died.

Eventually in Buffalo, marketing drummed up another radio "first" which, much like KDKA in Pittsburgh, has now been celebrated so long nobody seems to question it. May 22, 1922 is often marked as the anniversary date for the start of Buffalo radio.

That's the date WGR signed on. WGR promoted its first broadcast as "the birth of Radio in Buffalo" when the station called itself "Buffalo's First Licensed Broadcasting Station" during the station's 25th anniversary year in 1947. By the mid-50s, that had been shortened to "Buffalo's First Radio Station."

First, let's be clear. WGR did something Charles Klinck didn't. WGR was a licensed commercial radio station, and the first successful radio station to survive-- but it wasn't the first.

But back in 1922, WGR was not claiming that their broadcast was the birth of Buffalo radio-- because that would have sounded foolish to the people who'd been listening to Buffalo radio for years by then. Not only had folks listened to Klinck, but they also listened to another licensed station— WWT, which signed-on before WGR.

WWT had a host of technical problems and had nowhere near the support, staff, and finances that WGR had as an arm of the Federal Telephone and Telegraph Co.-- but WWT, not WGR, was Buffalo's first licensed station, for better or for worse.

Again, WWT disappeared when WGR signed on, and was mostly forgotten to history—to the point where nary an eyelash was batted when WGR "forgot" about the station 25 years later.

So the question remains…*when should we mark the start of broadcasting in Buffalo?*

It's hard to say. Like most technological advances, the early days of radio were more about experimentation and evolution rather than definitive dots on a timeline.

To fix that, I don't think we should erase dots—just add a few more and celebrate them all.

The research and writing presented in this book adds a few more dots on Buffalo's broadcasting timeline, and reclaims some rich history that's been long forgotten. It simply means more dates, stations, people and great moments in Buffalo broadcasting that are worthy of celebration.

Combined, they make for a full, rich history of a medium that has been a part of our lives—and reflective of our lives-- in Buffalo for a century now.

The earliest days of Buffalo broadcasting

History has set the start date of "The Radio Era" at November 2, 1920—when Pittsburgh's KDKA Radio went on the air with the world's first commercial broadcast, announcing the returns in the Presidential election that pit Ohio Senator Warren Harding against Ohio Governor James Cox.

History books don't usually mention that Buffalo was on the air that night, too.

The Buffalo Evening News had set up a special direct telephone line to the home of amateur radio operator Charles Klinck, who was teacher of electrical science at Technical High School and was able to fund his expensive radio hobby a member of one of Buffalo's top meat packing families.

After months of experimentation, he invented and pioneered the use of equipment that would allow for the clear transmission of phonograph records over his wireless transmitter.

"Well boys, how did you like that?" said Klinck, quoted in the Buffalo Courier after playing Strauss' The Blue Danube. "Now listen, and I'll give you a little jazz."

That was the sound, on a March night in 1920, in the attic at 38 West Parade Avenue, as America's first disc jockey took to the airwaves. You pass over the historic spot where it happened when you drive the outbound Kensington as you pass the Science Museum.

CHARLES KLINCK, JR. AT HIS WIRELESS

Klinck received word from as far away as Long Island that people were listening to his broadcasts. By mid-September, he reported that he was getting music requests from folks all over the northeast.

He also reported that from the beginning, the folks at the big wireless station in Pittsburgh were among his "most interested listeners." Months before that "first broadcast," the Westinghouse engineers at KDKA were tuned into Buffalo. On that Election Night 1920, Klinck was on the air from 6pm-midnight, offering election results interspersed with recorded music. Not only was he Buffalo's deejay, but also Buffalo's first radio newsman.

Charles Klinck, 1950

That first commercially sponsored broadcast in Buffalo was described the next day in The News.

As soon as the returns came into the Evening News office, they were telephoned over a special wire to Mr. Klinck's residence, where they were received by a member of the Evening News staff. From 6 o'clock until midnight, Mr. Klinck sat at his wireless telephone apparatus and sent out the encouraging Republican news. Not only were city and county returns flashed out over the wireless outfit, but also state and national figures.

During the evening, Mr. Klinck... received word from several wireless operators in the city, in Lancaster and surrounding towns that they were getting the returns by wireless with perfect satisfaction... During lulls between dispatches, the operators who were listening for the returns were entertained by musical selections from a Victrola in the Klinck home.

Listeners in Lancaster were amazed as the radio returns beat out the Western Union telegraph service by minutes. Pine Street druggist Harry Frost told The News that he enjoyed the "returns by wireless telephone" immensely. "We sat around very comfortably smoking cigars and commenting on the election, while every few minutes, Mr. Klinck's voice would roar out the results as he received them."

Both the technical aspects and the reaction to Buffalo's Election Night 1920 broadcast have been better chronicled than the "more historic" program the same night from Pittsburgh. The main difference remains that the KDKA broadcast was made by the Westinghouse Corporation in an effort to promote and sell the radio tubes they were manufacturing, while

Charles Klinck was an amateur operator without much interest in self-promotion.

When he died in 1978, his pioneering radio exploits went generally unremembered. The Courier-Express, for example, made no mention.

In the decades leading up to the radio era, many advances and discoveries that laid the ground work for radio happened in Buffalo.

In 1909, The Buffalo Evening News was a pioneer in wireless telegraphy, building one of the world's first wireless telegraph transmitting operations, Station WBL, on the fifth floor of The News headquarters building at Main and Seneca Sts.

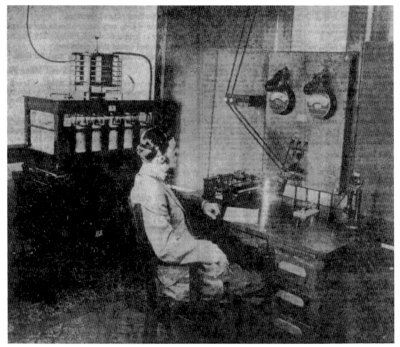

United Wireless Telegraph ran WBL from The Buffalo Evening News, 1909.

As early as 1924, a group of electrical engineers in Buffalo laid claim to having been the first to transmit and receive the human voice over radio waves in a series of experiments which took place at a Canisius High School laboratory in 1910.

John A. Curtin, later a professor at D'Youville College, reconfigured a primitive microphone to allow the voice to be transmitted and received over a wireless telegraph set.

The Canisius High School wireless set up, 1910

When Curtin said "A E I O U" into the microphone and across the airwaves, he might have become the first person to have their voice broadcast over radio. His voice was certainly the first broadcast in Buffalo.

About 18 months after the area got its first taste of commercial broadcasting with those election results, hundreds of people around Buffalo and Western New York tuned in their wireless radio receivers to hear the first broadcast of Buffalo's first commercial radio station, WWT, on Easter Sunday, 1922.

The station was the first in Buffalo to be licensed by the federal government, and broadcast regularly three times a week. "Every Wednesday and Friday night and on Sunday afternoons the apparatus will be used to send out programs of an entertaining or educational nature," reported the Buffalo Express.

Edna Zahn approaches the microphone at Buffalo's WWT studios on West Mohawk Street on the station's first day of broadcasting in 1922.

McCarthy Bros. & Ford company owned and operated the station from the third floor of its headquarters building across Mohawk Street from where the Hotel Statler was being built. From electric washers and sewing machines to wireless radio receivers, McCarthy Bros. & Ford was in the business of selling electrical appliances and luxury items.

McCarthy Bros. & Ford, the home of Buffalo's first radio station, WWT.

In order to sell radios, they needed to provide something for Buffalonians to receive on those radio sets.

That first transmission came at 3 p.m. on April 15, 1922. Buffalo's airwaves were christened with the sounds of "throwing a kiss across the ether," which was picked up in a radius of about 50 miles around Buffalo.

21

The lip smack of Genevieve Abraham kicked things off, followed by Buffalo soprano Edna Zahn and the piano accompaniment of Ethyol McMullen. These were the first sounds on Buffalo radio in the commercial era.

A look inside the WWT studios on the first day of broadcasting shows Ethyol McMullen, Edna Zahn and Edward O'Dea.

Edward O. O'Dea, who was later known as "Radiodea" on several Buffalo stations, was a sales manager for McCarthy Bros. as well as WWT's station manager and announcer for that first broadcast. Edward H. Striegel was the first engineer.

Easter prayers and songs were offered by Episcopal and Catholic clergy and choirs during that first Easter Sunday.

Buffalo Chamber of Commerce President Albert Kinsley spoke on that first broadcast about the wonder of it all.

"Had I ventured, only 200 years ago, to say anything of the kind might be done, especially in Salem colony, I probably would have been burned at the stake for witchcraft.

"We have become accustomed to modern miracles that they are accepted now as a matter of course.

"When ancients credited Jove with hurling thunderbolts, they may have had the nucleus of an idea, but certainly no conception that I the 20th century electric waves would be hurled 'round the world to carry the voices of mankind to serve our purpose.

"No man today can venture to limit the possible uses of this energy and probably none has the imagination to forecast its future.

"No one can say with certainty that we shall not yet step on a magic carpet of our own and be whisked where we wish to be with incredible speed."

Buffalo's first radio broadcast wrapped up with "Webb's novelty entertainers" sending the sounds of jazz through the city.

WWT was first, but wasn't alone very long.

On May 21, 1922, WGR broadcast its first programs from studios on the third floor of the Federal Telegraph Company on Elmwood Avenue, from a building that was the long-time home of FWS, and more recently has been renovated as the Foundry Suites and banquet facility.

Buffalo's first two radio stations, WWT and WGR, both signed on the air in an effort to sell more radios.

Having only been broadcasting for five weeks, WWT Station Manager O'Dea suspended broadcasting for the first week WGR was on the air, to

23

help avoid interference in WGR's signal, as had happened several times when WGR was running tests using the experimental call sign 8XAD.

Shortly after WGR signed on, WWT took a break from its schedule for the summer of 1922. The signal and the memory of Buffalo's first station faded away, mostly forgotten, into history.

As early as 1925, the Buffalo Courier ran a story asking readers if they remembered "old WWT," "from a time when broadcasting was young."

The earliest histories of broadcasting say that WGR was "Buffalo's first commercially viable radio station." When GR-55 celebrated 50 years on the air in 1972, the "commercially viable" part was dropped and they called themselves "Buffalo's First Radio Station."

WGR's first home was on the third floor of the still-standing home of The Federal Telephone & Telegraph Co. at 1738 Elmwood Avenue. The building to the left is now the home of The Buffalo Spree. A viaduct was created to remove the grade-level crossing of the New York Central Beltline railroad, which now stands at the left side of this photo.

If WWT's sign-on was met with a wholesome, "mom-and-pop" style fanfare, WGR's sign-on came with a corporate marketing blitz.

"Next Sunday Buffalo will enter into the field of national radio broadcasting with the formal opening of one of the largest and most powerful broadcasting stations in the east, which may make Buffalo the ethereal center of this part of the country," said the Courier.

WGR's first week was billed as "Radio Week," and each of Buffalo's six daily newspapers were given their own evening to fill with programming. Monday was the Buffalo Courier; Tuesday, The Buffalo Evening News; Wednesday, the Buffalo Times; Thursday, the Buffalo Express; Friday, the Buffalo Commercial; and on Saturday, the Buffalo Enquirer.

An ad for a program from WGR's first week on the air in 1922. The station isn't mentioned, but there was only one on the air in Buffalo at the time.

The scheme assured a week's worth of heavy promotion from the newspapers.

"(T)he Federal Telegraph & Telephone Company… has spent thousands of dollars to furnish Buffalo with a class of radio service which will be equal to that of stations which have been broadcasting since interest in radio began to assume such proportions," reported the Courier.

L. R. Weller was the operator and announcer for WGR's first broadcast. After prayers in Latin and then English from Rev. Michael J. Ahern, President of Canisius College, the first broadcast on WGR continued with addresses from Dr. Julian Park of UB and Rev. F. Hyatt Smith.

WGR's first studio, 1922.

Buffalo Chamber of Commerce President Albert Kinsey was also among the first to step to the WGR microphone, and tell of Buffalo's praises to radio listeners picking up the station in a 700-mile radius around Buffalo.

"He spoke of the great epoch of progress through which Buffalo is now passing and cited many instances of Buffalo's material growth," according to the Enquirer wrap-up of that first broadcast.

The station's powerful signal was not only good for promoting Buffalo, but for promoting radio in Buffalo. Signals from amateurs and WWT were often weak and spotty and required expensive receivers to listen comfortably.

WGR's first transmitting set, 1922.

The $25 set available from the owners of WGR radio could easily pick up the station within a 30-mile radius of the city.

"This renders radio reception in homes of Buffalo and vicinity no longer and instrument of the well-to-do, but for almost anybody who cares to use it."

Radio had become a much more affordable hobby, but it was by no means cheap. Charles Klinck's set-up was valued at about $5000 in 1920, which is more than $60,000 in 2020 dollars. That makes the $25 receiver much more affordable by comparison, but that price tag approaches $400 in 2020 dollars.

One trendy way the wealthy took to listening to the radio was as a railroad passenger. The Lackawanna Railroad heavily advertised that passengers could listen to WGR on the Buffalo Limited and the New York Limited.

"These train concerts are probably the most difficult type of radio work yet attempted," bragged a Lackawanna ad. Below, the train's radio receiver.

In May, 1923, WGR moved its broadcasting facilities from Elmwood Avenue near Hertel to become among the earliest tenants of Buffalo's brand new Statler Hotel. These studios were on the hotel's 18th floor. That space would later become the home of WBEN from 1930-1960.

29

The WGR staff getting ready to broadcast the 1924 Republican Convention: R.D.H. Nichols, operator; Milo Gurney, ad manager; Edward Stanko, operator; W.A. Rigg, studio manager; and T.A. Doddridge, operator.

Nichols, Doddridge, and Stanko in the WGR Statler Hotel control room, along with F.S. Martin, district manager for Federal Radio.

WGR was a licensed as a Class B station, which authorized it to broadcast on reserved frequencies, without interference from other stations, at high power. That meant the station could be heard regularly within several hundred miles, but could also be heard on occasion as far away as Hawaii and England. The special license also barred WGR from playing "canned music," meaning only live performances were heard on Buffalo radio during the earliest years of regular broadcasting in Buffalo.

Another seller of radio equipment, Howell Electric, started WEBR Radio in 1924. Herbert H. Howell's shop and station were located at 54 Niagara Street.

"With two stations in Buffalo operating alternately," reported The Enquirer, "it will be possible for the radio fans to hear programs anytime during the day."

Engineer John F. Morrison built and operated the station, the range of which was much more limited than WGR. Even through there were surprise reports of the station being picked up in Syracuse during tests, the intention was to "more fully serve local interests" with its programs.

WEBR's sign-on stunt involved station owner Howell (right) broadcasting over the station with instructions meant for Leslie Irvin— the parachute pioneer, who was flying in a plane above downtown Buffalo with pilot E.M. Ronne.

When Howell "directed the airmen where to

send their machine," the Courier reported, "almost simultaneously with the word of instruction the plane flew right and left, up and down."

The station also initiated "the Sunshine Radio Club," which was meant for radio fans to make a donation to help buy radios "for hospitals, orphan asylums, invalids, cripples, or, perhaps, a man who made a great sacrifice for you and me on the fields of France."

After six months on the air, the station doubled its power as it moved from Niagara and Franklin to the top floor of the Bramson Building, the home of Marine Trust Bank on Main Street.

The new 11th floor studios and more powerful signal meant another Buffalo station was among the small, but growing handful of large stations operating across the country.

After several test broadcasts, the station received a letter from a new "regular listener" 1,200 miles away in Norman, Oklahoma.

Children visit WEBR's Uncle Ben program, 1935. The boy furthest to the left is Gerhard Lang, nephew of the Lang Brewery owner, who was a regular junior announcer on the show after having told a bedtime story on the station's first day of broadcasting. The large round object, draped in black bunting is the microphone, hidden to help relieve the anxiety of performers, unaccustomed to such devices.

The World Series was heard in Buffalo in 1925 over Station WMAK (as seen on the microphone), with Associated Press telegraph operator Charles Wiest reading each play as it came over the cable from Pittsburgh. This night, the Pirates beat the Senators in Game 2 by a 3-2 final.

In Lockport, Norton Laboratories began operating WMAK Radio in 1922, with I.R. Lounsberry as the chief engineer and manager. Lounsberry's name would be associated with Buffalo radio right through the rock 'n' roll era as President of WGR.

WMAK became associated with The Buffalo Evening News, after The News broadcast election results on the station shortly after it signed on.

The station became more and more Buffalo-centric in its broadcasting, and in 1925, studios were opened in Buffalo's Lafayette Hotel in association with the Buffalo Times newspaper.

Shortly after the studios opened, in October 1925, Associated Press telegraph operator Charles Wiest announced play-by-play action of the World Series in Pittsburgh under the direction of the Buffalo Times.

Wiest read the telegraph cables over the air moments after they happened on the diamond.

In 1926, WMAK's place in history was secured when the station joined a "remote control broadcast chain" of stations across the northeast and Midwest in "an precedented demonstration" of "radiating a program" in nine cities simultaneously.

WMAK-Buffalo, WGY-Schenectady, WJZ-New York, WTAM-Cleveland, WHAM-Rochester, WFBL-Syracuse, WRC-Washington and Other Big Stations Join in Great Broadcasting Chain That Will Bring the World's Best Radio Entertainment to Buffalo Radio Listeners

It was the world's first network program, and the network that would grow from that first network broadcast was the Columbia Broadcasting System, CBS.

A pair of 60-foot radio towers stood atop Seneca Vocational High School until 1953.

Seneca Vocational students put on a radio drama over the WSVS airwaves, 1930s.

WSVS was another early Buffalo station, signing on in 1926. The studios were operated by the students of Seneca Vocational High School, and while many private high schools and colleges around the country received special licenses to broadcast, Buffalo's Seneca High was the only public high school in the nation with a fully-licensed radio station.

Students at Seneca Vocational School learned the engineering and maintenance side of radio in classrooms as a part of the educational operation of WSVS.

When WSVS first signed on, many of its programs were on par with the commercial broadcasters of the day, with a heavy schedule of bands, orchestras, signing groups and soloists.

Through the years, WSVS' broadcasts became more intermittent and more school-centered, as the station eventually shared the frequency of commercial broadcaster WBNY.

By the time WSVS surrendered its license in 1942, it had already been allotting near all of its broadcasting time to WBNY for years. Still, it was the last of the early educational stations to leave the airwaves, and the milestone was celebrated as *the silencing of a pioneer* in a national trade magazine.

Another selection in the long-forgotten alphabet soup of early Buffalo radio call letters is WPDQ. The station went on the air from the garage at 121 Norwood Avenue, owned by Nelson P. Baker (no relation to the Lackawanna priest.)

Garage owner Nelson Baker, upper left, WPDQ co-owner Hiram Turner at the controls, Frank Miller in the WPDQ studio at the microphone, 1925.

The station was on the air for one day—December 30, 1925—before the federal government suspended its license. The station eventually made it back on the air, broadcasting from the Varsity Theater on Bailey Avenue, until the station was sold and the call letters changed to WKEN and the studios moved to the corner of Delaware Avenue and Sheridan Drive.

WKEN also had regular broadcasting capabilities from Kenmore Presbyterian Church at Delaware and Hazeltine Avenues in Kenmore, and from the Great Lakes Theatre on Chippewa Street in Buffalo.

A federal rule change called barred some stations from being in residential areas, so the studio moved once again. This time literally.

The small building which was the home of station WKEN was taken by barge from Tonawanda to Grand Island in 1928.

The small building was wheeled up Sheridan Drive to the Niagara River, and then floated on a barge to Bush Road on Grand Island.

Right: WKEN broadcast nightly stock report information, sponsored by an investment house in the Ellicott Square Building, 1930.

The callsign for WKEN was lost to history when The Buffalo Evening News bought the rights to its radio frequency and allowed the station to go dark, before signing back on as WBEN in September 1930.

WKEN

Every
Nite
5:30 to 5:45

New York Curb report and a five-minute discussion on money matters by

The Investment
House of

Berner, Smith & Co.

Ellicott Square
BUFFALO

From the moment WKBW first signed on, November 7, 1926, the evangelist owner Dr. Clinton Churchill said the randomly assigned call letters stood for "Well Known Bible Witness."

Churchill came to understand the power of radio when his earlier broadcasts on WMAK and WEBR brought in bushel baskets filled with requests for more preaching, more music, and assumedly, a couple of dollars mixed in as well.

The preacher turned his Main Street Tabernacle building into a radio studio—it would later be the home of Channel 7.

"CT" inscribed on the studio seating for shows like Dialing for Dollars didn't stand for "Commander Tom," but for "Churchill Tabernacle."

The Churchill Tabernacle's Great White Robed Chorus ready to perform from what would become, 30 years later, audience seating for WKBW-TV shows like Dialing for Dollars.

WKBW Radio's first studio, 1926.

As radio became more popular and businessmen around the country began to realize ways of making broadcasting lucrative and profitable, to that end a handful of wealthy Buffalonians moved to bring together Buffalo's radio stations under a single umbrella.

In 1929, a million-dollar corporation was formed by a group of Buffalo bankers and businessmen to create the Buffalo Broadcasting Corporation—known informally as the BBC.

Buffalo Broadcasting Corporation

"The Voice of Buffalo"

Operating Radio Stations

WKBW WGR WMAK WKEN

485 Main Street, at Mohawk

Buffalo, N. Y.

April 1, 1929.

Linking WKBW, WGR, WMAK and WKEN promised "a vision of Buffalo as one of the country's largest radio broadcasting centers."

The directors of the new company included Marine Trust President George Rand, Western Savings President Charles Diebold, Jacob Schoellkopf, Irvine Kittinger, and Clinton Churchill.

"Nothing musical in Buffalo will be beyond the reach of the corporation," said Churchill. "We will produce the very best in radio broadcasting, technically and artistically.

"We will maintain staff orchestras, bands, musicians and soloists, and we win immediately set about to eliminate the cheaper and undesirable types of programs."

When the BBC was incorporated, it left WEBR as the lone independent station on Buffalo's radio dial.

But not for long.

S.S. Wallace, Master of Ceremonies and announcer for the BBC, early 1930s

Oklahoma Hank and his Western Entertainers, on broadcasting on WGR with a BBC microphone.

Station personnel from WGR and WMAK as published in a national radio almanac, 1927.

Prince Edward, Later King Edward VIII, dedicating the Peace Bridge in 1927.

In 1927, WGR made world history by hosting the first international remote broadcast of its kind when the Peace Bridge was dedicated.

A "great network" of stations in the US and in Canada agreed to transmit the address simultaneously for the first worldwide broadcast ever attempted. It was heard from Britain to Australia.

The Prince of Wales, who would later become King Edward VIII, was the featured speaker in the program for the nearly 100,000 spectators who lined both sides of the Niagara River, which also featured Vice President Charles Dawes, British Prime Minister Stanley Baldwin, Canadian Prime Minister Mackenzie King, and New York Governor Al Smith.

Graham McNamee and Milton J. Cross, the top announcers for the National Broadcasting Company, were in Buffalo for the historic broadcast.

As New York Governor and then later as President, Franklin Delano Roosevelt was no stranger to Buffalo and its microphones. Here, a speech by Gov. Roosevelt is being picked up by Buffalo Broadcasting Corporation microphones.

As a pioneering and early developing radio market, many of the talented people who helped shape the medium here in Buffalo through the 1920s moved on to fame and success outside of Western New York and became pioneers not just in Buffalo radio, but pioneers influencing the entire future of the medium.

Buffalo & The Lone Ranger

"The Lone Ranger," the first of many national radio serials with a Western flavor, was first broadcast on WXYZ Detroit in 1933, but it was a Buffalo man-- who first put the character on the air in Buffalo-- who was the creative force behind the program.

Fran Striker grew up in what's now the Elmwood Village neighborhood, attending Lafayette High School and UB during those post-WWI years when radio grew from fad to part of life.

His radio talents were first put on display as a musician in the earliest days of WGR in 1922, then moving to WEBR as an announcer when that station began broadcasting in 1926. There, as a writer, producer and program director—he was also responsible for selling the programs he wrote and performed in to advertisers.

Right: Frank Striker in 1928

It was on one of those WEBR programs where the character that would become famous as "The Lone Ranger" first appeared. "Covered Wagon Days" ran on WEBR in 1930.

The show was created, according to a 1930 Courier-Express article, after President Hoover authorized the "commemoration of the heroism of the fathers and mothers who traversed the Oregon trail to the Far West."

"This proclamation," the brief article continues, "was the inspiration for a new series of programs from the versatile pen of Fran Striker, which he has entitled Covered Wagon Days. One of them is heard from WEBR every Monday night. In them Mr. Striker gives listeners at that time a radio drama version of many of the interesting and exciting happenings which took place in the long and dangerous treks across the plains and mountains."

When Striker moved to Detroit, the character came with him and became a sensation. For much of the next 20 years, the Buffalo native wrote not only the radio scripts, but the newspaper comics, novels, and more in the voice of the hero who entered on "a fiery horse with the speed of light, a cloud of dust and a hearty *Hi-Yo Silver*."

In 1936, Striker was also a part of the team that created "The Green Hornet" character for a radio serial before that character also branched into comic books and film.

Still writing the daily comic strip, Striker moved back to Buffalo and was working to relaunch *The Lone Ranger* when he was killed in a car accident in 1962.

Lone Ranger and Green Hornet creator Fran Striker at home in Buffalo, 1957.

Striker wasn't the end of Buffalo's connection to the American cultural icon.

Jay Silverheels, the actor who played the Lone Ranger's companion Tonto, was a Mohawk born in Southern Ontario.

When he was 19, the man who would become famous as Tonto and his cousins moved to Buffalo to play professional lacrosse for the Buffalo Bowmans at the Broadway Auditorium-- where he was also a Golden Gloves boxer.

Born Harry Smith, the actor earned the nickname Silverheels in Buffalo— when new shoes helped him run so fast, *all you could see where the silver heels running across the field.*

Harry Smith was a boxer and professional lacrosse player when he lived in Buffalo in the 1930s. Later, using the stage name Jay Silverheels, he became famous for his role as the Lone Ranger's companion Tonto.

As handsome as he was fast, when Smith moved to Los Angeles in the late 30s to play lacrosse, he was quickly cast in films-- first as a stunt man and extra, then in 1949 as Tonto.

Stoopnagle & Budd

F. Chase Taylor (Col. Stoopnagle) and Wilbur "Budd" Hulick were announcers for the Buffalo Broadcasting Corporation at WMAK Radio in 1930 when Hulick was on the air and the CBS Network feed went down.

With 15 minutes to fill and nothing prepared, Taylor dragged an old organ into the studio, and the two went back and forth in character, using the kind of silly banter that they'd been doing around the station off-air.

F. Chase "Stoopnagle" Taylor and Wilbur "Budd" Hulick, 1932.

The pair quickly became Buffalo's most talked about radio personalities, and their WKBW program "Ask for Mail?" had people sending letters and listening for their chance at fame on the show.

In 1931, their "extemporaneous buffoonery" caught the network's attention.

"The Gloom Chasers" final Western New York appearance before heading to New York to fulfill that new network contract was a series of sold out shows at Shea's Buffalo—in a deal personally arranged by Michael Shea.

Stoopnagle & Budd became among radio's first high-paid national personalities, appearing on their own programs, in movies, and on the Vaudeville circuit.

After the act broke up, both men appeared on programs in both acting and emcee roles in the earliest days of television. Hulick returned to Buffalo in 1947 and hosted radio and TV programs with his wife Helen. The couple interviewed Lucille Ball and Desi Arnaz when Jamestown-native Ball visited on a mid-50s trip to Western New York.

Taylor continued to appear as Stoopnagle and write for television shows until his death in 1950 at the age of 52.

Roger Baker

One of the original superstars of Buffalo Radio in the 20s and 30s for the Buffalo Broadcasting Corporation's WGR and WKBW, Roger Baker was the Queen City's first definitive sportscaster. His 40-year announcing career started when he was a musician sitting in the orchestra waiting to go on the air, but no announcer showed up. He stepped up to the microphone and never stepped back.

A pioneer in the art of baseball play-by-play-- before him, calling the action of a baseball game was assigned to which ever announcer was next on the schedule. He was Buffalo's first regular baseball announcer, and gained recognition for his descriptions of Bisons games.

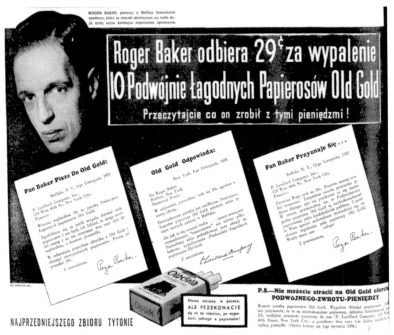

Roger Baker's play-by-play abilities transcended language. In 1935, his endorsement of Old Gold Cigarettes was translated into Polish and appeared in Dziennik Dza Wszystkich, Buffalo's Polish language daily newspaper.

Those who remember him in the sports booth remember the ultimate professional– no focus on personality, so much as the product on the air. His work from Offermann Stadium was straight and by the book.

After being tapped by Baseball Commissioner Kenesaw Mountain Landis to call the 1933 World Series to a nationwide audience on CBS, Baker was called up to the big leagues in 1939, replacing Red Barber as the voice of the Cincinnati Reds when "the Ol'Red Head" moved onto critical acclaim as the voice of the Brooklyn Dodgers and then the New York Yankees.

Deco Restaurants were an early sponsor of sportscasts in Buffalo, including Roger Baker's play-by-play broadcast of the Buffalo Hockey Bisons from the Peace Bridge Arena in Fort Erie in 1933.

In 1948, Baker returned to Buffalo as the news-reading General Manager on WKBW Radio. He eventually moved into the same news-reading General Manager spot at the short-lived Buffalo UHF pioneer WBES-TV Channel 59.

Along with Bill Mazer, Baker was also an original member of the WGR-TV sports team when the station signed-on in 1954.

"Years of experience covering sports events plus constant study of the sports picture account for the mature nature of Rog's evening sports telecast. Master of play-by-play, his reporting of sports as they happen has set the pattern for imitators all over the country," read a promo piece from the sign-on of Ch.2 in 1954.

When Clint Buehlman first stepped to the mic as a newly hired junior announcer for the Buffalo Broadcasting Corporation in 1931, he made waves with his silly programs where he was known as the station's "Chief Nutcracker." By then, the 20-year-old was already a radio vet, having acted on WGR dramas through the 1920s. He literally grew up and grew old with Buffalo radio and its listeners. Over his 46-year professional career, Buehlman became known for his little songs about driving in the rain and school closings. He'd start waking up Buffalo with WGR's Musical Clock show in 1932 and though he moved to WBEN in 1943, he'd continue hosting a morning radio show without interruption until 1977.

The Buffalo Evening News promotes its radio coverage in a booklet promoting its radio station, WBEN, in 1931.

Decorated in green and white, an early WBEN studio on the 18th floor of the Statler Hotel, 1930.

WBEN- The Buffalo Evening News Station

The Buffalo Evening News had been a pioneer in the field of wireless communications, from wireless telegraph station WBL which operated from The News headquarters, to setting up the radio relay of election results on "radio's birthday" in 1920.

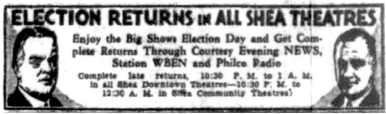

Even by 1932, there were still enough Buffalo homes without radios that the Shea's theaters around the city were open to broadcast WBEN's returns of the Presidential election between President Herbert Hoover and New York Governor Franklin D. Roosevelt.

"A new voice of the city is on the air, bespeaking new hopes and hoping to fulfill new opportunities for the entire Niagara Frontier," read the opening sentence of the story in The News, celebrating the initial broadcast of WBEN on September 8, 1930.

WBEN's first announcers in 1930 were, standing, William Cook, Merwin Morrison, and Bob White (also known as Chief Announcer Gorson Higham.) Seated are Edward Obrist and Louis Kaiser.

"Through the magic of radio, it expects to become an increasingly powerful factor for knowledge, for culture, for good citizenship."

The voice of announcer Merwin Morrison was the first to be heard on WBEN, but that first broadcast was opened with the playing of the Star-Spangled Banner, followed immediately by "the Maple Leaf Forever," which was then the national anthem of Canada.

WBEN's Blue and White Trio was a salon group that played music during the dinner hour in the station's earliest years. Shown in 1931 is director and pianist Karl Koch, violinist Charles Coumont, and cellist Frank Kuhn. Here, they are shown inside Buffalo's Elmwood Music Hall.

Buffalo Mayor (and Broadway Market butcher) Charles Roesch stands before the WBEN microphone at the Elmwood Music Hall to open Buffalo's Centennial celebration in 1932.

Buffalo Evening News Managing Editor Alfred H. Kirchhofer gave an address welcoming the listening audience to WBEN on behalf of the paper on that first day.

It was Kirchhofer, who would eventually serve as President of WBEN, who was more instrumental than anyone else in the paper's move to start operating a radio station, and then later to develop FM and television broadcasting stations as well.

"We can promise you that we will be our own most severe critics and that nothing shall interfere with the rapid development of a station that will be a credit to Buffalo and a joy to the listener," said Kirchhofer over the air that first night.

For the next 47 years, through the auspices of its newspaper owner, WBEN would be Buffalo's most thoroughly marketed and photographed radio (and later TV) station, as is evidenced on the pages of this volume.

WBEN broadcasting from the Buffalo River in 1936, with technician Earnest Roy, Buffalo Fire Captain Daniel J. Mahoney, announcer Lou Kaiser, and pilot Patrick J. Mulland. The men are aboard the fire boat "W.S. Grattan," which was renamed "Edward M. Cotter" in 1954.

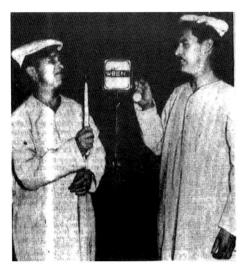

Earl Sheridan and Jack Doherty came to WBEN in 1935 as the Jack & Earl, The Minutemen from WYXZ in Detroit. Starting before the sun, they "broadcast popular songs, time signals, piano duets and comedy."

WBEN tried a long line of morning announcers in the 1930s, none of whom could put a dent in the popularity of WGR's Clint Buehlman.

Joe Wesp, WBEN's Ironic Reporter, spent much of the 1930s travelling to out-of-the-way places around Western New York and broadcasting live from those places. In 1936, his travels took him to Gowanda, where he spoke with 71-year-old Frank Davis in front of Gulley's drug store.

WBEN's first transmitter facility in Martinsville.

Roy Albertson's WBNY

Roy W. Albertson was one of the most colorful and divisive personalities in the history of Buffalo Radio—*and that's saying something.*

He came to Buffalo in 1921 as a reporter for The Buffalo Evening News, before hopping over to the Buffalo Times, where owner Norman Mack's Democratic politics were closer to his liking.

Albertson was elected secretary of the Erie County Democrats and after Mack sold the paper, Albertson moved over to WEBR where he became General Manager and on-air personality.

As WEBR's original and outrageous "Ye Olde Town Crier," with fire and determination he took on Buffalo's controlling Republican administration with weekly broadcasts that the Courier-Express called "pungent."

"He dispensed his thunderbolts in an era when yellow journalism was an art form and a little libel was looked on as the spice of life," reported The News years later.

He needled Buffalo Mayor Charles Roesch, referring to him only as "King Charles" and Roesch's appointed Police Commissioner Austin Roche "Lord Austin."

At one point, WEBR claimed that police were trying to interfere with the station's broadcasts—and from there on out, the Town Crier would broadcast from a different location each day.

In 1934, State Supreme Court Judge Alonzo Hinkley didn't like what he heard about the goings-on in his courtroom on Albertson's program—so he sent a sheriff's deputy over to arrest him and hold him in contempt of court. Albertson spent the night in jail and was found guilty—although the ruling was later overturned.

During his time at WEBR, Albertson applied for a license for his own new radio station, and WBNY signed on in March, 1936.

Among the station's first on-air staff was Ralph Hubbell, who would be celebrated for decades as the Dean of Buffalo's sports broadcasters. Even right out of the gate, he was popular on a new station.

Left: Ralph Hubbell left WBNY for Buffalo Broadcasting Corporation's WGR in 1939.

"Ralph Hubbell possesses every qualification for the job. A nose for news. An analytical mind. A nimble tongue. A thorough knowledge of all branches of sport. A wide and understanding acquaintance with all its leading personalities," said an ad from sponsor Kendall Motor Oil.

Buffalo's boxing champ Jimmy Slattery sent Hubb a note saying *he not only loved his sports commentary, but his reciting of poetry on the air as well.*

As part of the station's licensing process, Albertson promised WBNY would be "free of politics," but in 1940, an angry Mayor Thomas Holling had WBNY's line from the police headquarters severed and the station uninvited from city property after a program that the mayor called "a blitzkrieg" against his administration.

Albertson sold the station in 1958, and soon thereafter the call letters changed to WYSL. In 1966, WBNY-FM signed on in Buffalo at 96.1 FM—that station had no connection to the Albertson station.

President Roosevelt talks to reporters holding WBNY and WBEN microphones outside of Buffalo City Hall, 1940.

FDR in Buffalo as President

Only weeks before he was to be elected to his second term as president, Franklin Delano Roosevelt visited Buffalo to dedicate the city's new federal building at Niagara Square on Oct. 17, 1936.

The visit was Roosevelt's first time in Buffalo as Commander-in-Chief -- although he had visited countless times during his four years as New York's governor. The courthouse was a federally funded New Deal project and was designed primarily by Buffalo architect E.B. Green.

The president's dedication was carried on radio stations WKBW, WBEN and WBNY.

"I need not compare the Buffalo of today with the Buffalo as I saw it the last time I was here," Roosevelt said in Niagara Square. "You will recall, I am sure, those years when I had the privilege of being the chief executive of this state. Already in 1930 the problems of unemployment and depression had become severe and you will recall also that it was in 1931 that I, as governor, called the Legislature of the State of New York into special session to provide relief for the distressed unemployed of the state and New York was the first state in the Union to definitely accept the responsibilities of seeing to it that as far as the state's resources could prevent it, none of its citizens who wished to work would starve."

Wider view of President Roosevelt's 1936 address, with the Niagara Square side of the Statler Hotel seen prominently in the background.

"*We can't honestly say that Buffalo is the largest market in the country,*"
wrote the Buffalo Broadcasting Corporation in a 1936 ad in a national
magazine, "*But we can truthfully claim that it is one of the best and has
been consistently so for many years.*"

Philco radios
were among the
available in
1932, and The
Wm. Hengerer
Co. was selling
this seven-tube
model in the
downtown store's
seventh floor
radio shop for
$49.75-- which
amounts to just
under $900 in
2020 dollars.

Photos of the women of early radio are far and few between—and that's because unless they were singing, there just weren't many women on the radio during the first two decades. This 1933 photo shows Lillian Kaye, WGR's "crooning contralto." Her voice was heard regularly through the 20s and 30s on Buffalo radios and around the country on network shows on NBC.

The story of Clint Buehlman's first five years at WGR were told in a comic strip that was included in a booklet commemorating the milestone and distributed by the station in 1937.

The Hall Baking Company, sponsors of Clinton Buehlman's Musical Clock Show on WGR, was located in the large bakery building that would later be home to the Kaufman's Bakery on Fillmore Avenue at Main.

Following the Musical Clock Show, Buehly and technician Lew Shea would hop in the WGR Mobile Studio car for programs around town at places like Hengerer's and Shea's Buffalo.

Father Justyn's Rosary Hour

"If St. Paul were alive today, radio is the medium he would use," said Fr. Justyn Figas, who began his own Polish Language broadcast of the rosary in 1927 over WKEN, before creating a six-station rosary network in 1931 from Buffalo's WEBR. His broadcasts were heard in other cities with large Polish populations like Chicago, Cleveland, Detroit, Milwaukee, Scranton and Pittsburgh.

"I greet you dear friends, with the words 'Praise be to Jesus Christ.'"

The Franciscan priest's manner made him the perfect man to reach out across the airwaves; everyone at his Broadway-Fillmore parish of Corpus

Christi loved him. One parishioner remembered him as "stern but kind, always with a warm sense of humor."

Almost immediately, Fr. Justyn (also spelled Justin) was leading millions in Polish-Americans in prayer. And, almost immediately following his success, he was criticized in some circles for speaking in a foreign language on American radio and "promoting hyphenated Americanism."

With eyes keenly focused on his mission, he would often wear a coat or a hat that had seen better days. When kind people offered him a few dollars for a new hat, he'd gladly accept—but instead of a new hat, he'd put the money towards one of his many projects-- like building St. Joseph Hospital in Cheektowaga and St. Francis High School in Hamburg.

He became a world-renown broadcaster, but first and foremost, he was a Franciscan—caring deeply about every person he encountered. Despite growing fame and responsibility, he always exuded joy while taking on the mundane physical tasks of running a parish community.

Fr. Justyn hosted The Rosary Hour for 31 years until his death in 1959.

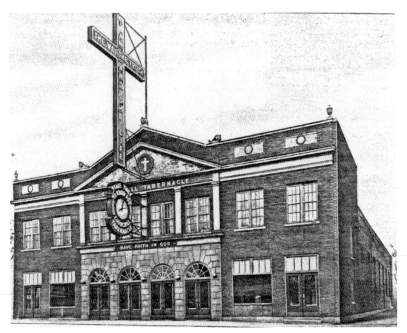

Sacred organ music was broadcast over WKBW and Rev. Clinton Churchill preached on "One Thing Every Sinner Should Know," on the day when four new electric signs—including a 30-foot red-and-white porcelain cross—were dedicated in 1937 at the Churchill Tabernacle at 1420 Main Street.

The new cross was the gift of Pastor Churchill in memory of his mother and in honor of his father. Hanging beneath the cross, a large sign and two illuminated electric clocks.

The building became WKBW-TV's Television Center in 1958, and remained Ch.7's home until moving to the current location at 7 Broadcast Plaza in 1978.

The wall on the right side of the photo was the first home of Tom Jolls' "Weather Outside."

Airing weeknights at 11 on WGR from 1938-46, Mr. QED was one of Buffalo's most listened to radio news programs. QED was actually Hamburg High School history teacher Edward T. Schweikardt. The program came to an end when Schweikardt was offered a professorship at Toledo University. When this ad ran in 1940, Manru's Schreiber Brewing was one of at least nine local breweries operating in Buffalo.

Buffalo Police Commissioner Austin Roche was an early proponent of radio, first as a means of outreach—he wrote and starred in a weekly "crimelogue" program on WKBW.

A strong believer in what radio could do for crime fighting, Roche pushed for the creation of Buffalo Police station WMJ, which signed on in 1931.

In 1936, the Border Patrol put radio to use to "tighten the gates of the Niagara Frontier."

WMMB was located at the foot of Arthur Street at the Niagara River. The 200-watt transmitter broadcast every half hour. Thomas McDermott, shown above, was the station's chief operator.

Among the hardworking staff in this BBC election night photo are Roger Baker (with cigarette at the typewriter) and Clint Buehlman (far right).

In the middle at the mic above, and in the photo below is "effervescent emcee" Cliff Jones, "your aireporter." The Nichols grad joined WGR in 1935 and later was heard on WBEN, WHAM in Rochester, and WBTA in Batavia.

Stations on the move

The 1940s started with most of Buffalo's radio stations changing their dial positions.

The governments of the US, Canada, Mexico, Cuba and Haiti signed a treaty agreeing on a realignment of the radio dial in 1940.

It meant that five Buffalo radio stations got new frequencies in a continent-wide attempt to clear up interference in the increasingly busy airwaves.

Lower end frequencies, like WGR at 550 kilocycles, weren't forced to move, but in December, 1941, WBEN moved from 900 to 930 kilocycles, WEBR from 1310 to 1340, WBNY from 1370 to 1400 and WKBW from 1480 to 1520. WEBR moved again in 1945 to 970, putting Buffalo's AM stations in the same dial locations where they still are today.

WGR and KB are also broadcasting from the same transmitter facilities eight decades later.

The Buffalo Broadcasting Corporation opened its transmitter and tower facilities in Hamburg on Big Tree Road in July, 1941. The facility cost $350,000-- $6.1 million in 2020 dollars—and was described as "truly a showplace of electric marvels."

The WKBW-WGR Transmitter facility on Big Tree Rd. as it looked when opened in July, 1941.

When the building first opened, a series of telephone lines carried programs from the Rand Building studios of WGR and WKBW to Hamburg for broadcast.

The Buffalo Broadcasting Corporation newsroom of WGR & WKBW inside the Rand Building.

WKBW's mainstays were the network programs of CBS with stars like Orson Welles, Hedda Hopper, Cecil B. DeMille, and Kate Smith. WGR carried the Mutual Network featuring "The Lone Ranger" and Milton Berle.

The local talent celebrated in a brochure issued in commemoration of the new transmitter included Billy Keaton, Ralph Hubbell, and WGR Orchestra leader David Cheskin. Before Howdy Doody came along, Bob Smith hosted "The Cheer Up Gang" every morning, and before spending Clinton Buehlman hosted "WGR Musical Clock."

Clint Buehlman, host of WGR's Musical Clock

The 50,000 watt signal which erupted from this building provided the coverage across much of the eastern part of North America which WKBW Radio to become, as their top-of-the-hour IDs would say during the Jeff Kaye era, "One of America's two great radio stations."

A technician adjusts the audio driver tubes of WKBW's transmitter. 1941.

Herb Rice was WGR's program director and the station's creative force from 1929-43. He was an integral member of the Stoopnagle & Budd team, and was among the first to display the talents of Buffalo Bob Smith in 1933. In leaving Buffalo to become an executive producer for NBC, Rice worked with and wrote for Bing Crosby, Bob Hope, and Katharine Hepburn.

Buffalo's first look at TV

Buffalo's first television station, WBEN-TV Channel 4, did not officially sign on until 1948. But eight years earlier, Edwards—the department store at Main, Mohawk, and Genesee-- hosted Buffalo's first transmission and reception of "Farnsworth electronic television" signals from inside the store.

See a Complete Demonstration of **MODERN TELEVISION . . . Be Televised Yourself Without Charge,** of Course, and Receive a Television Test Certificate.

Continuous 15-Minute Program with Short Intermission Between Shows

THREE DAYS
Thursday, Friday, Saturday

Continuous Programs
No Admission Charge

Thursday beginning at 12 Noon . . . Friday at 11 A. M. . . . Saturday at 10 A. M.

History in the Making

Comparable to the thrill of seeing your first automobile or first airplane! Not an experiment, but a complete Farnsworth Mobile Electronic Television unit in operation.

Hear and See

programs originated in the fully equipped studio — hear and see them televised—hear and see them reproduced on the Farnsworth studio control screen.

Farnsworth

is the great name in television, the man whose dreams made possible electronic television which reproduces images just as sharp and clear as you see them on the finest movie screen.

Special Broadcast! Come to Edwards and hear AND SEE SALLY WORK broadcast over WBEN and be TELEVISED in our store Friday Morning at 9:45 A. M.

Come! See and Hear the FIRST Buffalo Television Demonstration THURSDAY, FRIDAY and SATURDAY on Edwards Lower Floor . . . No Admission Charge!

Hear AND SEE the WBEN News Flashes broadcast over WBEN and TELEVISED in our store Thursday, Friday and Saturday at 12:30 P. M.

Seeing moving pictures on a small piece of glass for the first time must have been some sight, "comparable to the thrill of seeing your first automobile or airplane!"

Buffalo's radio staff musicians

The WGR Staff Orchestra, featuring conductor David Cheskin, right. Announcer John Lascalles is at the microphone to the left.

The best known and most remembered musician of Buffalo's radio staff musician era is probably Dave Cheskin.

He was a "one man wonder" during the Golden era of Buffalo radio in the 30s and 40s, serving as WGR's Music Director, band leader, and conductor.

Trained at Juilliard and then a violinist for the NBC Orchestra for three years, Cheskin came to Buffalo as the music director for the Erlanger Theater, soon taking on the role of Buffalo Broadcasting Corporation Music Director in 1931.

His live broadcasts, conducting the 18-piece WGR Orchestra, were among Buffalo's most popular radio programs of the day.

At one point, Cheskin was also conducting 18 network shows a week— including "Buffalo Presents"— heard all over the country on NBC and CBS as performed live in the WGR-WKBW studios.

Cheskin was tapped as the Buffalo Philharmonic's Pops Conductor through the war years, and spent more than 30 years leading one of Buffalo's premier dance bands.

The members of Cheskin's bands and orchestras also move on to their own high-profile radio gigs as well.

Harold Austin, known for leading the bands at the Crystal Beach Ballroom and on the Crystal Beach boat "The Canadiana," as well as in the Dellwood Ballroom during WEBR's Hi-Teen Show, started his musical career as a musician in Dave Cheskin's WGR Orchestra.

Through the years, hundreds of thousands of Buffalonians waited at the foot of Main Street to board The Canadiana. Once aboard, the sound of Harold Austin's Orchestra filled the ship in the 30s, 40s, and 50s.

Violinist Max Miller was a featured star for many years with the WGR Orchestra, until he was named WBEN's Musical Director.

Miller was nine years old, the first time he played the violin on Buffalo radio. After graduating from Buffalo's East High School, he played regularly as a part of the Shea's Buffalo orchestra.

Max Miller, center with violin, leads the WBEN Orchestra.

Miller took over the reigns at WBEN from Bob Armstrong, the trombone and cello player who'd lead the WBEN-NBC Orchestra for most of the 1930s.

Bob Armstrong's Hotel Statler Orchestra in 1941 (above) was mostly the same group heard on WBEN at the time.

Vera Holly and Herman "Tiny" Schwartz were the featured vocalists, sitting at the front of the stage.

The musicians included, in the front row, Charlie Wullen, leader Bob Armstrong, Bill Jors, John Porejko, Stan Zureck, John McFadden, and Bill Wullen. In the second row, Pat Vastola, Dan Brittain, Hank Krompart, and Andy Dengos, with Ed Rydel and Tom Sist at the top of the bandstand.

The Federal Theater Jubilee Singers on WEBR in 1938. From left to right, Ruth Malone, Grant Johnson, Martha Boynkin, Robert Edwards, Harriett Baull, and Godfrey Tottin. The group was unit of the Depression-era WPA Federal Theater Project. They travelled the city to portray the origin of Negro spirituals and jubilee music.

The winners of WEBR's 1940 "Barbershop Harmony" contest were James Davies, Daniel Colley, Crawford Anderson, and Donald Rowley.

*Clare Allen was WEBR's jack-of-all trades through the 40s, 50s, and 60s—
as a newsman, emcee, quizmaster, and on-air outdoorsman-- but also chief
announcer, program director and promotional director. During the 31
years that WEBR was owned by the Courier-Express, Allen also became a
prolific writer for the newspaper, chronicling changing face of Buffalo
through the 50s and 60s. Below, Chief Engineer Frank Ridgeway and
Allen load up the WEBR mobile van.*

It's Radio's Big
Two For One Bargain
T. N. T.
With
COLIN MALE
TIME, NEWS and TEMPERATURE
WITH T. N. T.
TIMELY, NEEDED, TERRIFIC
HOME APPLIANCES
6-9:45

Colin Male spent several years in the 1940s at WEBR before heading to Hollywood. He made a handful of television and film appearances as an actor, but the Bennett High grad is best remembered as the announcer who talks over the whistling on the opening credits of the Andy Grifftith Show.

Gomer Lesch was WEBR's "Doctor of Discography" and announcer on popular shows like "Queen City Cinderella," hosted by Clare Allen and Billy Keaton.

Lesch was a Riverside High School grad who left WEBR to navigate B-29s in World War II. Until his death in 2019, he often put his media skills to work for the Baptist church.

Through the 30s and 40s, Al Zink was one of Buffalo's most beloved radio hosts as the emcee of "The Children's Hour" on WEBR for more than 20 years. Many of those kids grew up to listen to him as the local host for NBC's "Happy Birthday" program. Here, "Uncle Al" gives $40 checks to Mrs. Edith Reardon and Mrs. Marie Walczak at the WEBR studios on North Street.

Zink was part of the WEBR staff under three different owners—founder H.H. Howell, The Buffalo Evening News from 1936-42, and the Buffalo Courier-Express, which bought the station from The News when Federal regulations changed, barring an entity from owning multiple stations in a market. The Courier-Express sold WEBR in 1972.

Ad from The Buffalo Evening News Almanac, 1941

The WBEN Players ham it up in studio for a 1942 performance.

WBEN's new Grand Island transmitter, 1943.

Before coming to WBEN in 1936, Ed Reimers worked at WHO in Des Moines, where he often shared the same mic with sportscaster—and later President—Ronald Reagan.

Reimers was WBEN's top announcer before joining ABC's announcing staff in 1948. Soon he was in Hollywood, working steadily in television's infancy.

He filled in as an announcer on NBC's Tonight Show—a gig arraigned by fellow WBEN alum Jack Paar, and was the regular announcer on Westerns Cheyenne and Maverick. His best remembered TV acting gig was on the original Star Trek series, where he played Admiral Fitzpatrick in the "Trouble with Tribbles" episode.

But it was *with hands cupped* he entered American pop culture consciousness. Reimers was the television spokesman and steady voice who reminded viewers, "You're in good hands with Allstate" from 1958-77.

Reimers, holding the script, is joined by WBEN personalities Dr. Frederick Hodge (seated), Esther Huff (center), and George Torge & John Eisenberger (far right) at a broadcast from Kleinhans Music Hall.

Announcer Aaron Levine was often heard on WGR and WKBW giving local station breaks during network programs and reading newscasts.

One of Buffalo's all-time sports reporters chats with one of Buffalo's all-time athletes. WGR's Ralph Hubbell talks with Bisons slugger Ollie Carnegie. Carnegie still holds the record for most games as a Bison and his International League all-time homerun record stood for 69 years. Both men are in Buffalo's Sports Hall of Fame.

While the show has been best remembered as introducing Helen Neville to Buffalo, Laura Rischman was the original hostess of WKBW's "Modern Kitchen" show starting in 1938. Here, her smiling gaze is backed by the sour disposition of Buffalo Broadcasting Corporation's Night Manager Malcolm Barney. The show offering "practical help with dollar and sense values in nutrition and home management" was taken over by Neville when she arrived on the Buffalo radio scene from WBTA, Batavia in 1943.

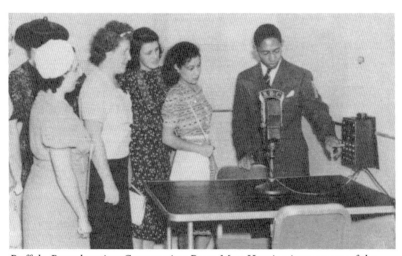

Buffalo Broadcasting Corporation Page Matt Harris gives a tour of the BBC studios, showing how an announcer turns his mic on and off.

Charlie Bailey was one of Buffalo's leading sports journalists for 40 years. A long-time Courier-Express sports columnist and WEBR personality after the paper bought the radio station, Charley Bailey's early radio career at WGR-WKBW was a varied one. He stepped into WGR as an assistant to Roger Baker in 1933, before joining the staff of the Courier-Express as a writer and columnist in 1942. He spent time behind the sports play-by-play microphone which would be his realm through the 1960s, but he also "donned a high hat and white tie for a survey of Buffalo's night life on "Man About Town."

Starting in 1946, Bailey was back on the airwaves at WEBR, and he would serve that station as sports reporter, play-by-play man, and Sports Director until the 1970s. An old school reporter, Bailey was tough but always smiling, and always seemed ready to turn the perfect phrase.

*"Bob Schmidt, so versatile that it is difficult for us editors," read the
caption on this photo in a pre-war publication for the Buffalo
Broadcasting Corporation.*

"Smiling Bob Smith" was how Masten High School grad Robert Schmidt
was known through most of his years on WGR from 1936-1944.

He also spent a couple of years at WBEN before moving onto New York
City to host the morning radio show on WEAF (later WNBC), and become
one of the great stars of the early days of television as Howdy Doody's
sidekick, "Buffalo Bob Smith."

Buffalo Morning Radio Wars, 1940s style

With city hall as a backdrop, WGR morning man Clinton Buehlman takes to the ledge of the Rand Building during his wake-up show to wake-up motorists in Lafayette Square, 1942.

Clint Buehlman signed on as WGR's morning man in 1932, and remained Buffalo's undisputed king of morning radio until his retirement in 1977.

For 11 years on WGR, and then for 34 years on WBEN, there was no more listened-to, beloved, or marketable voice emanating from Western New York radios.

Almost immediately and for all his 45 years waking up Buffalo, Buehlman was able to turn his own popularity into sales when he talked about a sponsor.

The combination of fawning listeners and fawning commercial clients are what every station manager *dreams of* in a morning show.

WBEN announcer and Sun Greeter Club emcee Al Taylor, 1941.

WBEN had been on the air for more than a decade with little headway in making a dent in Buehlman's dominance.

There was The Minute Men Show with Jack and Earl, and starting in 1938, emcee Al Taylor hosted the Sun Greeters Show on WBEN.

When Taylor—who interviewed Adolf Hitler as a newspaperman in the 30s—left for WCAU in Philadelphia, he was eventually replaced by a man The Buffalo Evening News called "silly… fast-talking… and glib," Jack Paar.

Jack Paar sits at a WBEN typewriter in 1942, writing jokes and serials like "Joyce Jingle, Girl House Detective." "She had a schoolgirl complexion," Paar wrote, "until it graduated."

"Jack is WBEN's Sun Greeter who rattles along at breakneck speed from 6:05 until 9 in the morning, playing records, reeling off nonsense, telling the time, dishing out choice morsels of Hollywood gossip and what-not just about the time you're eating your breakfast cereal," wrote The News.

Almost two decades after he left Buffalo, Jack Allen wrote about Jack Paar in the Courier-Express as the former Buffalo morning man celebrated his fifth anniversary as the host of the "Tonight Show."

The controversial host, at 25, patrolled the early morning for WBEN radio in 1942-43. His satirical quips 'woke 'em up' on morning radio as they now 'keep 'em up' on late-night TV. Paar entered the Army in 1943, to be succeeded on WBEN by Clint Buehlman.

Paar is remembered by some radio executives here as 'a talented personality who worked hard at original comedy' and 'despite his humility he is strongly egotistical.'

WBEN hired Clint Buehlman away from WGR in 1943 after Jack Paar left for the Army.

Buehly welcomed to the WBEN's Statler studios by Station Manager Edgar Twamley in 1943.

After a decade as the host of "The Musical Clock," WGR's morning show, in 1943 his new WBEN show was called simply "Clint Buehlman."

"That should be sufficient but, for the newcomers to Buffalo, it means time announcements, all types of music, jokes, and anything else that helps to make up a fast-moving show," explained The Buffalo Evening News.

"Clint is one of the few men who can work without script and whose ad-libs are funnier than many carefully rehearsed network programs."

"Fast-moving" and "funny" might not be the descriptors those who remember Buehlman in the 60s and 70s might use, but he grew up and grew old with us on the radio.

Toward the end of his uninterrupted 46-year run hosting Buffalo's top-rated morning radio program, Buehlman sounded like the cranky grandfather he was—reminding men to wear their rubbers and pay close attention to the road.

Still, even into his last decade on the air, more than half of radios that were on in Buffalo during the morning hours, had Clint Buehlman on. He may have been a crotchety grandpa, but he was the whole city's crotchety grandpa.

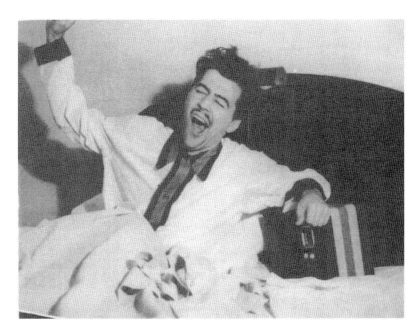

Buehlman was replaced on WGR by Foster Brooks--- who'd later be known to television viewers around the country for his routine at the "lovable lush."

Coming to Buffalo from WHEC Radio in Rochester, Brooks joined WGR/WKBW in 1943 as the emcee of the Musical Clock morning show Buehlman had made dominant, while also emceeing WKBW's "Million Dollar Ball Room."

Along with "Buffalo Bob" Smith and Johnny "Forgetful the Elf" Eisenberger, Brooks was the third member of WGR's "the High Hatters," a popular Country & Western vocal group. He was a late replacement trio after the original third voice left the group.

Brooks left Buffalo around 1950 after winning an Arthur Godfrey talent contest—but spent most of the next 30 years coming back to Buffalo through the magic of television—as a guest on both Steve Allen's and Johnny Carson's Tonight Show, numerous guest starring roles on shows like Adam-12, and many Dean Martin-produced shows like Martin's variety show and his celebrity roasts.

He became famous for his "Lovable Lush" routine, where he played hundreds of different characters who were so blotto they could barely stand—but didn't think their inebriation was noticeable.

The comic had given up the bottle by the time his act had become famous, but he later admitted while in Buffalo, there might have been times where he resembled the character that he'd made famous.

"I was very fortunate I didn't get in trouble," Brooks said in 1978.

"There were times I'd get home at 4, wake up at 5, and be to work at 6. I had to close one eye to read the news and the commercials. There were two and three words where there was only supposed to be one."

Fellow WGR announcer Ralph Hubbell—who wrote about his own public battle with the bottle in his book "Come Walk With Me"—would often drive Brooks home, and "Hubbell and my wife would explain who I owed apologies to."

Brooks stopped drinking in 1964, and his star took off from there.

Buffalo Radio at War

"Women's Army" aired on WGR to help with the recruitment of WAACs. Announcer Denny Schute interviews Lt. Jeanne Gatt from the WGR studios at the Rand Building.

Blackout drills were a way of life during World War II, and the first came the day after Christmas, 1941.

Radio stations set aside their programming to help conduct the drill. The following account was in The News the next day, and shows a tremendous overview of radio in Buffalo at that time.

"Only lights burning in most Buffalo homes Friday night were tiny dial lights on radios, while the radio stations that poured out a stream of information about the blackout were lighted themselves by small blue bulbs not much larger than those on listeners' sets.

"Although most stations possess "inside" studios which have no windows and thus could be kept as brilliant as possible, all preferred to switch out all lights except tiny blue ones near their microphones and technical-control panels.

"WBEN, whose studio windows in Hotel Statler were covered securely by wallboard shields, kept only a dim safety light burning in its inside "standby" studio where other announcers remained on duty while Ed

A WBEN billboard painted on a building behind Buffalo City Hall, 1944.

Reimers described the blackout from a 20th-floor vantage point in City Hall. Control room windows were likewise covered and dimly lit.

"Blinds were drawn completely over all studio windows at WEBR in Broadcasting House, 23 West North Street. A lone bulb glowed in one studio in use, and a tiny green light illumined control room switches and dials.

"Blue cellophane was fastened over control room lights, tiny meter bulbs were changed from white to red and only desk lamps were in use in two inside studios of WGR-WKBW, which linked to carry a description by announcers Jack Gelzer and Bob Sherry from an 18th-floor parapet of the Rand Building of Buffalo blacking out.

"Tight-fitting cardboard covered WBNY's windows in the Nellany Building and one blue bulb glowed in the control room and another in one studio.

"Visible from vantage points about the city were red warning lights on WBEN's transmitter towers on Grand Island, WEBR's tower on the Larkin Terminal Warehouse, WGR-WKBW antennas in Hamburg and WSVS' towers on Seneca Vocational High School.

"These warning lights must be kept burning at all times under federal law, unless ordered out by military authorities. The Civil Aeronautics Board ordered that aeronautical lights such as these must be kept burning during test blackouts. WBNY's tower in East Eagle Street carries no signal beacons, not being so required because of its location and height."

During the war years, stations offered plenty of patriotic programming. Several radio stations offered live coverage of the opening of the new Curtiss-Wright factory in Cheektowaga just before the US entered the war. It was the largest airplane factory in the country when it opened in 1941.

CURTISS-WRIGHT WORKERS
Tune in Tonight at 7:30 P. M.
Station WBNY---1400 ON YOUR DIAL
Hear DICK McCLELLAN, Rank and File Worker. Leaving Next Week for Service with America's Armed Forces

WKBW's "Commando Corps Court of Honor" was a program that encouraged young people to sell War Stamps and Bonds. Announcer John Boothby makes the announcement in the Lafayette Hotel Ballroom that the program had raised more than $330,000 by the end of 1942. To the right of the mic is Chief Announcer Jack Gelzer, who came up with the program. WGR-WKBW Announcers Robert Sherry and Jack McLean are also on hand.

In 1944, Buffalo's War Emergency Radio Service radio station signed on. WQWT was part of a nationwide network meant to operate using portable transmitters in the event of emergency.

WEBR engineer Ray Lamy oversaw the operation, which, had it ever been used, would have employed amateur operators using their own equipment—all in an effort to save resources for the war effort.

"Junked radio sets and parts, salvaged from cellars and attics, are being rebuilt by amateurs and professionals into two-way stations and operated for the public good," reported Popular Science in 1943.

Nominally meant as a means of communication during natural disasters, the system was built in anticipation of air raids on American targets. It was disbanded at the end of the war.

Buffalo's radio stations touted their war coverage in ads in the Courier-Express and The Buffalo Evening News daily through the years of the war, 1941-45.

The High Hatters entertain at Curtiss-Wright, 1944.

In 1946, the long-standing Buffalo Broadcasting Corporation partnership of WGR and WKBW was broken up, as WGR was purchased by a group led by longtime Buffalo radio man I.R. "Ike" Lounsberry.

Signing the paperwork to buy WGR are, seated: Edward J. Gorono, BBC counsel; Leo J. Fitzpatrick, chairman of the board of WGR, and I. R. Lounsberry, WGR president and general manager. Standing: Edwin F. Jaeckle, BBC counsel; Norman E. Nobes, WGR secretary-treasurer, and Raymond J. Meurer, counsel for WGR.

Lounsberry was there at the very beginning of radio in Western New York, as one of the engineers/operators/announcers who put WMAK on the air in 1922.

As he explained in 1931, "In 1922, it was one and the same person who operated the technical equipment, announced the program, booked talent, did janitor duty and numerous other tasks."

He stayed on when WMAK was absorbed into the Buffalo Broadcasting Corporation, and stayed with the BBC until he broke it up with the purchase of WGR for $750,000 in 1946.

108

Esther Huff (left) plugs her ears as Bob Smith reads his watch to time a screaming contest announced by Clint Buehlman (far right) on WBEN's "Early Date at Hengerer's."

Shortly after Clint Buehlman left WGR for WBEN, Smilin' Bob Smith followed. With Esther Huff, they co-hosted "Early Date at Hengerer's" live from the downtown department store. While Buehlman's pace was fast and his persona was slapstick, Smilin' Bob was more laidback and homespun.

Clint Buehlman works the room at Hengerer's downtown store on Main St.

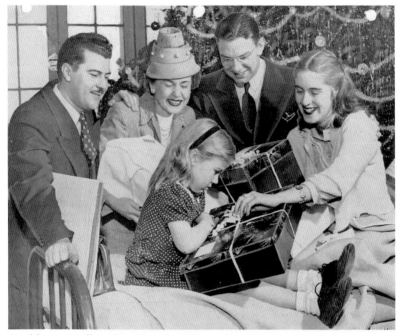

Buehlman, Huff, and Smith visit with a polio victim during Christmas.

Smith's routine caught the ear of NBC executives in New York City looking to build a team for the network's Big Apple flagship station.

Shortly after Smith left WBEN for the New York's WEAF Radio in 1946, longtime News and Courier-Express radio critic Jim Trantor wrote:

"Buffalo's Smilin' Bob Smith, who's become one of NBC's fair-haired boys on the New York scene... is going great guns at the head of a television show for youngsters down there and looks to have just about the rosiest future imaginable."

The show would become "The Howdy Doody Show," and Smith was destined to become one of the great early stars of television.

After Smith left, Les Barry took over his spot on the Hengerer show which ran through the 40s. The show moved and was eventually taken over by John Corbett—*Johnny from JN's* (JN Adam & Co. Department Store.).

The "gay and charming hostess" of the show, Esther Huff, began her radio career at WGR in 1927 with an afternoon show for women discussing fashion, homemaking tips, and Hollywood news.

Through the mid-40s, she was a regular on several WBEN programs.

Buffalo Mayor Bernard Dowd (light suit in the middle) and News Owner Edward H. Butler, Jr. (with pocket square) were among the dignitaries who signed on Buffalo's first regularly scheduled TV service.

WBEN-TV signs-on, 1948

For the few thousand with TV sets that could pull in the new station, the wait was excruciating.

On February 27, 1948, WBEN-TV started telecasting daily—but only a test pattern for several hours a day.

Eleven weeks later, on May 14, 1948, Buffalo entered the television era with the sign-on of Ch.4, WBEN-TV. The station was among the first 25 to sign on in the country.

"Edward H. Butler, editor and publisher of The Buffalo Evening News, stepped before a WBEN-TV camera at Memorial Auditorium on May 14, 1948—and a new era in mass communications and home entertainment began on the Niagara Frontier," read an announcement from the station.

The station's first-day, four-hour lineup offered a taste of what television would be like over the next couple of years in Buffalo—a little bit of everything.

After the somber address by Mayor Dowd and Mr. Butler, there was a Town Casino Variety Show, including the Town Casino chorus, acrobatic dancer Dorothy Deering, and network singing star and emcee Mary Jane Dobb.

The Town Casino chorus—"The Adorables," entertained on Ch.4's first night of broadcasting. The high-kicking ladies were Barbara Stafford, Alice Noonan, Jerry MacPhee, Gini Ruth, Melhi Jestrab, and Lee Borger.

And the show that would be the station's most popular for the next decade was also on Ch.4 that first night —There was wrestling live from Memorial Auditorium.

WBEN-TV cameras in Memorial Auditorium.

"The marceled master of mayhem, Gorgeous George, will take over the spotlight when the tele-cameras shift to the auditorium's wrestling ring at 9:30," read Buffalo's first TV program guide.

Just as radio had been a truly pioneering experience 25 years earlier-- with no one exactly sure what to do because no one had ever done it before, the first few years of programming at Ch.4 were an exciting and *sometimes weird* hodge-podge of adapting things that worked on radio for television mixed with completely new ideas for the completely new medium.

South Buffalo's Fred Keller, who first joined WBEN as an announcer in 1942, was the creative spirit behind many of the shows on Ch.4.

Mary Jane Dobb was the emcee and Dorothy Deering performed acrobatic dancing on a Town Casino Variety Show on Ch.4's first night on the air. Behind the camera is Program Director Fred Keller, who was also a writer and announcer that evening. "Radio Mirror" called him "one of the top television idea-men in the East." Among his credits was the creation of Ch.4's beloved Santa Claus show.

Because sponsors meant more than format, Chuck Healy's "Iroquois Sports Spotlight" show hosted Buffalo Zoo Director Joseph Abgott and his monkey friend "Mike" visited when the zoo opened the Iroquois Monkey Island.

Remembered as a sportscaster from the day WBEN-TV signed on in 1948 through 1977, Chuck Healy was also Buffalo's most watched TV news anchor on Ch.4 through the '60s.

The versatile announcer was also a versatile athlete as a boxing and football star at Syracuse University.

"Clowns and tigers" sounds more like a bad dream than a TV show. There was no caption attached to this photo, but based on the cameras without WBEN-TV stenciling, it was probably taken in early 1948, well-before the station signed on with a regular schedule.

At 9:30 on Wednesday mornings, the Czurles family hosted "Woodland Crafts, as a part of the "Live and Learn" summer series on Ch.4. Dr. Stanley Czurles was the Director of Art education at Buffalo State Teachers College.

Another of Ch.4's most popular early shows The TV Barn Dance, sponsored by Hal Casey's South Park Chevrolet. At various times, the show featured country musicians who were also known as around Buffalo as disc jockeys-- Art Young, who was heard on WXRA and WKBW, performed with his group the Borderliners. Lee Forster, who hosted shows on WEBR, WKBW and WWOL, performed on the program—and also met his wife on the Ch.4 sound stage.

Ailing veterans gather around a brand-new television set in the recreation lounge of the VA Hospital in Batavia in 1949.

*Ed Reimers interviews singer and bandleader Vaughn Monroe on Ch.4,
early in 1948, while the station was still experimenting and not yet
broadcasting a full schedule.*

"Studio D," on the Statler's 18th floor as Ch.4 presents "The Clue," perhaps the best remembered of Ch.4's live, locally produced dramas.

Television's first ever cop drama, "The Clue" was written and directed by Buffalo theater icon Fred A. Keller, and starred Evening News Radio-TV columnist Jim Trantor as *Private Eye Steve Malice*. It was as an actor on "The Clue" that Canadian radio announcer Lorne Greene—later famous as Ben Cartwright on Bonanza—made his first television appearance.

Stuart Roth and Jim Mohr recreate a scene in Ch.4's "The Law & You."

Brothers Jim (above) and Don Trantor lit up 1920s Buffalo radio with their piano act "the 20 Fingers of Melody." Don was later the TV and Radio critic for the Courier-Express, while Jim was the promotions director for the WBEN stations. As shown above, he also played "Steve Malice, Private Eye," starring in Ch.4's "The Clue."

It took a cast and crew of 22 to put on a 15-minute episode of "The Clue," including Director Keller, Writer Wander, Ass't Director Baldwin and announcer Bob Nelson. Actress Nadine Fitzpatrick is flanked by Trantor, Conrad Schuck, Charles Dempsey and Keith Hopkins. The technicians include Neil O'Donnell, Frank Holliday, Arthur Graff, John Knoerl, Gordon Pels, Gee Klumpp, Chet Pardee, Doug McLarty, James Kane, John Hagmman, Donald Stilwell, and William Noble.

Jim Trantor was also one of Ch.4's early news men. He was the host of the weekly Iroquois Illustrated Press, which took a longer look at the week's top news stories.

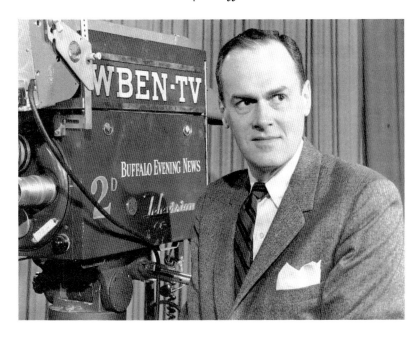

Harry Webb (above) and Ed Dinsmore (below) were Ch.4's most seen news anchors during the station's first decade on the air.

*Celebrating Ch.4's fourth anniversary in 1952 were Harry Webb, Bill
Peters (who played Santa Claus from 1954-72 as well as "Norman
Oklahoma"), and "Uncle" Jerry Brick, who was a Ch.4 floor director
when he wasn't hosting a kid's variety show.*

*Chuck Healy's easy and professional manner was a Ch.4 mainstay from
the day the station signed on until 1977. Strictly a sportsman in the early
days, Healy would be Buffalo's most watched news anchor in the 1960s.*

Director Gertrude Noble and Floor Manager William Noble look on as Victor's Amateur Hour emcee James Trantor rehearses a commercial with producer James Christensen.

Woody Magnuson was another of the hosts on WBEN-TV's Amateur Hour, this time sponsored by North Park Furniture. He was also the host of a longtime WEBR kids show as "Uncle Bill."

AHK

Starting in 1927, Alfred H. Kirchhofer spent 39 years at The Buffalo Evening News as the Managing Editor then Editor. He was also Vice President, then President of WBEN from 1930-67.

AHK (as he referred to himself) or Mr. Kirchhofer (as everyone else referred to him) was the man in charge of WBEN Radio before there was a WBEN Radio.

His influence was key in the News' purchase of the station in 1930. From 1927 until his retirement in 1967, Kirchhofer ran and expanded a News Empire that included The Buffalo Evening News and added WBEN Radio in 1930, in 1936 added WEBR Radio (then a News property), WBEN-FM in 1946, and WBEN-TV in 1948.

Despite his founding of four broadcast outlets, Kirchhofer was first and foremost a newspaper man. After joining the Buffalo Evening News in 1915, he opened the News' Washington Bureau, and became a familiar figure to Presidents Harding, Coolidge, and Hoover, all the while being Buffalo's eyes and ears in the nation's capital.

Realizing the potential for radio beyond selling newspapers, Kirchhofer developed a staff of radio writers and newsmen for WBEN and put the station on top to stay for decades.

The FM and television stations developed under Kirchhofer were not only Buffalo's first, but among the first in the nation.

Even as much of the broadcasting world reflected the changes in society through the 50s, 60s, and 70s, the staunch conservative content and dry delivery at the News Stations was a direct result of Kirchhofer's editorial approach.

His News style book included a section titled, "avoid mentioning hideous creatures." Rats and snakes became rodents and reptiles. Women weren't "pregnant" but *with child* on the pages of The News, and "motherhood is not treated as a situation comedy."

The approach made the News Stations "The Stations of Record" for generations.

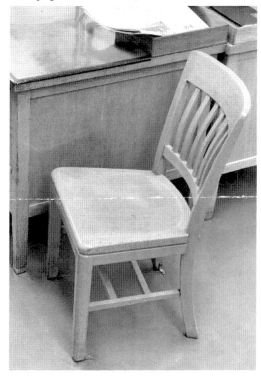

Another famous Kirchhofer story involves the chair next to his desk, which was notoriously bolted to the floor, nominally as a way to keep "boozy salesmen and politicians from getting too close," but in practice, it was an intimidation tactic for anyone speaking with him.

Elda Lucente broadcast the Italian Hour on WXRA in 1949. The station was founded in Kenmore in 1947, and sold to become WINE in 1957.

The 1947 WGR announcing staff consisted of chief Allen Lewis (seated), and David Getman, Bernard Ryan, Robert Sherry, and Don Gill.

Bob Glacy joined the WGR/WKBW staff in 1938. In the early 40s, he hosted WKBW's "Headlines on Parade" morning news program. He was the long-time host of "Glacy's Basement" on WKBW and through the 50s, was one of the stable of hosts and disc jockeys at WGR.

Over the more than 15 years Bob Glacy spent at WGR Radio and later WGR-TV, he did just about everything from newscasts to disc jockey to hosting Ch.2's TV Dance Party.

Later on WEBR, he hosted "Coffee Break" between 10 and noon from the fourth floor Civic Room of the downtown Sample Shop at 554 Main Street.

"Glacy will be seated in a glass studio shaped like a coffee-maker. Shoppers will be able to watch the broadcast and have coffee and rolls. Relaxed music will be geared to the housewife and home-bound office worker."

CHVC signed on from a studio next to the Rainbow Bridge in Niagara Falls, Ontario in 1947. The station offered some of the first programming created by Black Western New Yorkers meant to be listened to by Black Western New Yorkers. Johnny Thomas and Flora Henderson produced programs on CHVC meant for an audience in Buffalo.

"The Quiz of Two Cities" on WBEN pitted the people of Buffalo vs the people of Rochester, with Wally Nehrling, quizmaster.

The Buffalo Bills of the AAFC, 1946-49

Jim Wells, who left WBEN for nearly all of World War II to broadcast for the Navy in the South Pacific, returned to the station in 1946 as WBEN Sports Director.

In 1948, he left broadcasting and joined the team—becoming special assistant to the owner for the Buffalo Bills of the All-America Football Conference.

George Ratterman was a four-letter man at Notre Dame and the star quarterback of the Buffalo Bills from 1947-49, throwing 22 touchdowns his rookie year. When the AAFC folded, several of its teams moved to the NFL—but not the Bills. Ratterman moved on to several NFL and CFL teams before studying law and becoming the legal counsel for the American Football League Players' Union. His broadcasting career began at WKBW in

1950. Through the 60s and 70s, he was a color commentator for AFL and NFL games on ABC and NBC. He might be best remembered in the booth for his longtime partnership with Jack Buck.

Among his early assignments when Bill Mazer came to Buffalo in 1947, was to call the play-by-play of Buffalo Bills Football at the War Memorial Stadium for the 1940s incarnation of professional football in Buffalo.

Bennett High's future star power, 1946

Bennett High School's class officers in 1946 included John Otto (front row, leopard tie) and Sorrell Booke (standing, far right).

Buffalo Broadcasting legend John Otto was the 1946 Bennett High School Class President, but he was not the radio star of the class.

While he did appear on WGR as a ten-year-old accordion player on Major Bowes' Amateur Hour in 1941, Otto didn't become a familiar voice in the night (on the radio, on the telephone) until after serving in the Navy following graduation.

The class valedictorian Sorrell Booke had already been appearing in locally produced radio dramas for more than a decade, won a contest on WGR with his impersonation of Hitler, and was considered a regular actor on WEBR by the time he was a sophomore at Bennett.

Booke-- the man who would ultimately be best known for playing Boss Hogg on TV's The Dukes of Hazzard-- was a classically trained actor who attended Yale by way of Bennett High School.

When Sorrell was 10, he began his radio career by hopping on a street car, heading downtown to the Rand Building and asking for an audition on WGR. He wound up with steady work as an actor in radio dramas through high school.

For most of the 50s, 60s, and 70s, Booke saw steady work as a character actor playing roles on more than 200 TV shows before landing the starring role on The Dukes, which he called "gravy after a long career."

John Otto's broadcasting career began as a disc jockey and newsman on WBNY Radio, before moving to WGR, where he spent most of the 1960s as a "jack-of-all-trades" on both WGR Radio and WGR-TV Ch.2. Otto hosted children's shows, was a TV weatherman, and hosted a local TV talk show, as well as the radio work that he'd be best known for, starting with a program called Extension 55 on WGR.

Remembered for his brilliance, class, and unparalleled ability to put the English language to its best possible use on live radio, Otto died in 1999, still hosting his "nighttime conference call of all interested parties" as many as six nights a week.

After "The Dukes of Hazzard" ended its seven-year run in 1985, Booke continued to act in guest starring roles on shows like "Newhart" and "Full

House," while also becoming quite prolific as a voice actor on animated children's shows.

For his part, he never let the fame get to his head. After seven years of playing Boss Hogg on TV, Booke once told a reporter, "I'm not a jet-set type. I'm just an ordinary guy from Buffalo."

More than 175,000 people packed into the Delaware Park Meadow for a 1948 WBEN/Buffalo Evening News July 4th Celebration featuring Bob Hope, who presented a $6000 check to Moir Tanner of the Children's Hospital Endowment fund from the News Charity Fund.

WBEN announcer Gordon Redding is joined by engineer Edward Czech at the Buffalo Water Intake pier, reporting on how Buffalo gets its drinking water.

WBEN announcers Ed Wegman, Gordon Redding, Les Barry, Budd Tesch, Fred Keller, Woody Magnuson

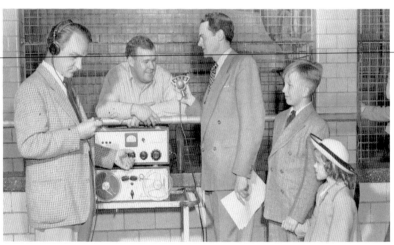

Harry Webb came to Buffalo from Schenectady as a classical music announcer on the new WBEN-FM, and wound up spending 24 years on TV. Webb was Ch.4's first newscaster, when the broadcast days began at 12 noon, and involved reading the latest edition of the Buffalo Evening News to an audience of several hundred. By the time Webb retired from newscasting in 1972, he had seen and been a part of the change of television from an indulgence of a few wealthy families to a modern global apparatus and definitive of disseminator information. Here, with technician Ed Huber, he records a show at the Buffalo Zoo.

WBEN announcers Don Cunningham, Ralph Hubbell, Jim Gardner, Harry Webb, Bill Weatherly

UB Roundtable, first presented on WBEN Radio and then on Ch.4, ran for nearly 40 years. This edition from the early 40s featured UB's Dr. Earl McGrath, Dr. Harry Rockwell of the State Teachers College, Dr. Samuel Capen of UB, and Msgr. Timothy Coughlin of Canisius College.

After hosting "Listen While You Lunch" on WEBR right after the war, Tap Taplin was the host of WEBR's early morning "T-N-T Show" in the early 50s. "Let him remind you about the time and temperature. There are news reports at 6, 7, 8, and 9 for information about the day's events... and last, but not least, Tap plays your favorite recorded music." Later, he spent time at WBNY.

Jack Eno first appeared at WEBR's "Ye Olde Town Crier" in 1935. After some time at WGR-WKBW in the 40s, Eno returned to WEBR for a more-than 20-year run starting through the 50s into the 70s. In this shot, John Clark in playing the records in the control room.

WEBR's daily Queen City Cinderella show, with announcer Gomer Lesch and emcee Clare Allen, awarding prizes to housewives and making one... Queen City Cinderella for the day.

Bob Wells came to WEBR in 1946 to create a music and dance show to help keep kids out of trouble. Hi-Teen became one of the most popular radio shows in Buffalo history, and Bob Wells one of the most beloved stars of radio and later TV.

WEBR morning man Chuck Cook enlists the help of Queen-O Beverages and a model to find "Buffalo's Hottest Corner," during a summer heat wave in 1949.

John Boothby was an announcer at WGR-WKBW in early 40s, and became WEBR's wartime chief announcer while also working at the Curtiss-Wright plant.

Ed Little's 62-year radio career included a stop at WBEN immediately following service in the war, and then a lengthy stay as one of WEBR's top announcers, emcees, and disc jockeys.

Billy and Reggie Keaton

Billy Keaton in the WGR studios with singer Johnny Ray.

Like many of radio's pioneers, Billy Keaton's foray into the medium came in the pre-war days when he adapted his Vaudeville routine for WEBR, and then into the highly popular "Stuff and Nonsense" program on WGR.

His success turned a temporary Buffalo assignment permanent. After the war, Billy's wife Reggie joined the act, and the two hosted the "Mr. and Mrs. Show" for a decade.

AROUND THE
BREAKFAST TABLE

with

THE KEATONS

(REGGIE & BILL)

9:15 A.M.
TO
9:50 A.M.
MON. thru FRI.

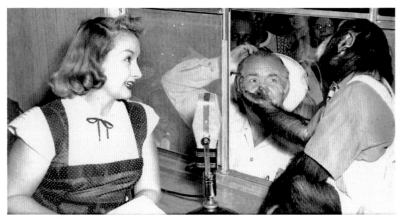

Reggie and Billy interview a monkey.

While the Keatons' voices were familiar throughout the '40s and '50s, their faces were soon popular as well. As a long-time WGR Radio fan favorite, Billy was the natural choice to welcome the first viewers to WGR-TV in 1954. The Keatons later hosted several cable TV talk shows through the years, leaving a legacy of 55 years of entertaining Western New York.

Reggie Keaton panics as her husband Billy gets ready to lay a smooch on a cardboard cutout of starlet Linda Christian during the couple's show in the WGR studio.

Sally Work spent the bulk of her radio career on WBEN, but was a pioneering Women's Editor on WGR starting in 1926 first. By 1948, her show carried 15 sponsors and a waiting list out the door.

The WGR Flashcast

In 1940s America, the frenzied commercialism, hot-burning bulbs and pulsating neon of Times Square ignited a sense of wonder and excitement over what an American city could be.

Buffalo had its share of the lights – Main Street near Chippewa was aglow with what was described as "Buffalo's great white way," and the greatest

TONIGHT AT 9–MAIN & COURT

TIMES SQUARE *Comes to Buffalo*

WGR BROADCASTING CORP.

and

THE WESTERN SAVINGS BANK OF BUFFALO

BRING YOU *FLASHCAST NEWS*

UP TO THE MINUTE HEADLINES IN MOVING LIGHTS

Tonight at 9 p.m., Mayor Bernard J. Dowd, Council President Peter Crotty and the members of the City Council will officiate at the inauguration ceremonies of the new FLASHCAST NEWS SIGN at Lafayette Square. The public is invited.

display of dazzling and flashing marquees and signs between New York and Chicago.

One lighting element Buffalo didn't have – until 1949 – was a flashcast news sign. WGR Radio was the sign's sponsor, which meant in red neon, those call letters brightly bookended the revolving ribbon of news headlines at Main and Court streets from atop the Western Savings Bank building. Visible from the WGR studios across Lafayette Square in the Rand Building, the scroll was controlled from WGR's newsroom.

While the sign was promoted as Times Square coming to Buffalo, the event to throw the switch on the sign, hosted by Mayor Bernard Dowd, was called a "Hollywood premiere-type event."

A few months after the first messages started streaming across the lights, a News story talking about improvements being made downtown mentioned the sign. "Here is a group of men at Main and Court streets, looking up at the Flashcast. They're squinting a little to read the moving electric words in the sunlight."

By the time WGR Radio's studios had moved to the building behind Ch.4 at 2065 Elmwood Avenue in 1959, the sign had gone dark. It had been completely removed by 1962 when construction was started on a new $4.5 million, 12-story Western Savings headquarters next door.

Ralph Hubbell

As already mentioned, his first radio job was reading poetry over the brand new WBNY, where he also became the station's sportscaster in 1936.

Ralph Hubbell started as WGR's sports director and moved on to WBEN in 1948, becoming "The Dean of Buffalo Sportscasters" along the way, "displaying a quick wit, warm personality and mastery of language."

Ralph Hubbell at WGR's news desk with chief announcer Jack Gelzer

In 1948, he was Buffalo's first TV sports anchor, although the term hadn't been invented yet. He was in the booth for the first few seasons of Bills football. Youngster Van Miller was on the play-by-play, but Buffalo's good sports fans loved the steady observations of Hubb during the games.

Charley Bailey of WEBR, Jim Wells of WBEN, Sig Smith of WKBW, and Hubb were Buffalo's top radio sportsmen of the 1940s.

When Hubbell retired after 58 years in Buffalo broadcasting in 1989, Buffalo News Sports Editor Larry Felser, a legend in his own right—grew up listening to Hubbell, remarked "those familiar vocal cords… always seemed to have been freshly dipped in motor oil."

Just ask "Yours Truly, Buehlly!"

"Loblaw bakers make 'em g-o-o-d!
They rush 'em to you f-r-e-s-h!
And they taste d-e-l-i-c-i-o-u-s!
BUY Loblaws baked goods T-O-D-A-Y!"

So says the discerning bard of Buffalo, WBEN's Clinton Buehlman, one of the nation's top radio entertainers ... heard every weekday morning from 6:00 to 9:00.

Loblaws FRESH APPLE PIES

These pies are filled with fresh sliced apples, delivered fresh every day from the orchards along Lake Ontario. Combined with cinnamon and nutmeg to give it that right taste for good eating—plus, a flaky, melt-in-your-mouth crust.   ea. **49ᶜ**

APPLE KUCHEN   Made with Fresh Apples   ea. **29ᶜ**
ALMOND RINGS   Fruit Filled, Danish Pastry   each **45ᶜ**

BLACK WALNUT
Layer CAKES

This is a delicious golden cake filled and covered with a rich black walnut butter cream icing, chuck full of ground black walnuts.   ea. **59ᶜ**

Typically, each 15-minute segment of Clint Buehlman's daily broadcast was sponsored by a single business. In the earliest days, as outlined in this ad, "Your AM-MC" would not only talk conversationally about that sponsor and its services and products, but also sit at the piano and sing songs about sponsors, weather, news and just about anything else.

By the time Buehlman was forced into retirement at age 65 in 1977, his days of sitting at the piano were long gone — replaced by adult contemporary music that could be heard all over the AM dial in that era. But between records, Buehly still would mix weather, things you needed to know and a few words from his sponsor, just like he had for the previous four decades.

From the 1949 *Buffalo Area Radio-Television Guide,* here are some of the names and faces from radio stations just outside of Buffalo. Stations included are Lockport's WUSJ, Olean's WHDL, Niagara Falls' WHLD, and WJTN & WJOC, both from Jamestown.

In 1950, television bore little resemblance to what beams into our homes so many decades later.

The test pattern was a regularly scheduled part of the broadcast day, which on most days didn't start much before noon.

Still, the growing number of television sets and the wonder of it all was putting dents in the entertainment powerhouse of the previous three decades.

"Radio, facing stiff TV competition, continues to seek means of holding its position in program ratings during the evening hours," wrote the Courier-Express in 1952.

Among the general similarities between then and today is the popularity of sports on TV. But Buffalo's favorite television sports in 1950 were live and local.

WBEN-TV Programs Next Six Days

Monday, Jan. 16

10:00-12:00—Noon—Test Pattern
2:00 to Sign On —Test Pattern
3:55—TV Showcase—program preview
4:00—Homemakers Exchange
4:30—Test Pattern
5:10—TV Showcase, program preview
5:15—Judy Splinters (NBC)
5:30—Howdy Doody—Sustaining
5:45—Howdy Doody—Mars Candy (NBC)
6:00—Shoppers Guide
6:30—Sports Spotlight, with Chuck Healy—Special Half-Hour Program from March of Dimes Sports Dinner, Hotel Statler—Sears, Roebuck & Co.
7:00—Kukla, Fran & Ollie—RCA Victor Puppet Show (NBC)
7:30—INS Newsreel—M & T
7:45—Camel News Caravan (NBC)
8:00—Chevrolet Tele-Theater "The Voice of the Cricket" (NBC)
8:30—Voice of Firestone, with Helen Traubel, Howard Barlow's Orch. (NBC)
9:00—Lights Out — Admiral suspense drama—Jack LaRue, narrator (NBC)
9:30—To be Announced
10:00—Studio One, Josephine Hull in "Give Us Our Dream"—Westinghouse
11:00—FBI Fugitives
11:10—Hambleton Sports Review
11:15—O'Keefe's Weather Forecast

Tuesday, Jan. 17

1:00 to Sign On—Test Pattern
3:55—TV Showcase
4:00—Homemakers Exchange (CBS)
4:30—Test Pattern
5:10—TV Showcase, program preview
5:15—Judy Splinters, (NBC)
5:30—Howdy Doody—Wander Co. (NBC)
5:45—Howdy Doody—Colgate-Palmolive-Peet (NBC)
6:00—Test Pattern
6:25—TV Showcase—Clark Candy Bar
6:30—Meet the Stars, Lenny Page emcee—Town Casino
6:45—Sports Spotlight—Schreiber Brewing
7:00—Kukla, Fran & Ollie — Sealtest (NBC)
7:30—"The Clue," Stein mystery drama
7:45—Camel News Caravan (NBC)
8:00—Texaco Star Theater, Milton Berle and guests (NBC)
9:00—Let's Relax with the Four Quarters—Barcalo Musical
9:15—It's Fun to be Fooled—Bill Wahl, "Master of Mirthful Magic—Crosley
9:30—Life of Riley—Pabst comedy program with Jackie Gleason (NBC)
10:00—Old Gold Original Amateur Hour. Ted Mack, emcee (NBC)
11:00—South Park Chevrolet B a r n Dance, Art Young and Dona Lee
11:30—Hambleton Sports Review
11:35—O'Keefe's Weather Forecast

A look at two days' worth of programming on Ch.4 in 1950.

Wrestling from Memorial Auditorium

Starting in 1949, Friday night meant Ralph Hubbell, Chuck Healy, and TVs tuned to live wrestling from Memorial Auditorium—with the action and antics of folks like Gorgeous George, Ilio DiPaolo, Dick "The Destroyer" Beyer, Coco Brazil, and the Gallagher Brothers and dozens of others.

During pre- and post-match interviews, the athletic Healy would often find himself somehow entangled with the wrestlers he was trying to interview— handling the headlocks from "bad guys" with the grace of a professional broadcaster.

There's little question—especially in Buffalo, wrestling helped make TV and vice-versa in those early years.

In 1951, Ed Don George was promoting wresting in 30 cities, including Buffalo. "Let them try to besmirch the wrestling profession as much as they'd like," said Ed Don, "But what other form of sporting entertainment gives as much to the fans as wrestling?"

He was proud of wrestling's showmanship, which had blossomed since he had been the world's heavyweight champ 20 years earlier. "Sure, there is showmanship in wrestling. We try to dress up our business just like the downtown merchant decorates his shop windows to attract customers."

Wrestling, of course, goes way back in Buffalo. Crowds sold out Friday night matches through the 30s, 40s, and 50s; first at the old Broadway Auditorium (now "The Broadway Barns" and the home of Buffalo's snowplows) and then Memorial Auditorium when it opened in 1940.

"This was a shirt and tie crowd," said the late Buffalo News Sports Editor Larry Felser, who remembered when Wrestling at the Aud was one of the biggest events in Buffalo.

151

"Not that many people had TV sets back then," remembered Felser in 2001. "People were crowding into Sears and appliance stores to try to see this thing on TV, because the place was sold out."

And with all those big crowds, there was no wrestler who could draw them in like Gorgeous George.

"When Gorgeous George would wrestle, they'd pack the Auditorium for this guy," said Felser.

"The Human Orchid," as George was known, was the first modern wrestler, said retired Channel 7 sports director Rick Azar, saying he "changed the face of professional wrestling forever."

As someone who called himself "Hollywood's perfumed and marcelled wrestling orchid," it's clear that George knew how to make sure he set himself apart.

"He had an atomizer, and he'd walk around the ring with perfume, supposedly fumigating his opponent's corners," said Felser, who also remembered George's flair for marketing outside the ring.

"His valet drove him around in an open convertible around Lafayette Square, and he's got a wad of one-dollar bills, and he was throwing money to people. It was a show stopper. He landed on page one. TV was just in its infancy then, but they were all over it. It was like World War III. That's how big a story it was."

Gorgeous George is credited with ushering in the Bad Boy era of sports– and even inspired Muhammad Ali, who told a British interviewer, "he was telling people, 'I am the prettiest wrestler, I am great. Look at my beautiful blond hair.' I said, this is a good idea, and right away, I started saying, 'I am the greatest!'"

Wrestling was cheap, flashy and easy to televise — and Gorgeous George was the performer that people loved to hate. It was said that in TV's earliest years, Gorgeous George's appearance on TV sold as many televisions as Milton Berle's.

Another of TV's favorite early sports was bowling. Chuck Healy was the host of "Beat the Champ" through the 50s, 60s, and 70s. Nin Angelo and Allie Brandt would become among Buffalo's most popular athletes because of their feats of bowling prowess on the show. All-American Bowler Vic Hermann's family still proudly talks about the day Vic rolled the first 300 game in the history of the show.

Chuck Healy also hosted "Strikes, Spares, and Misses," Buffalo's show for lady bowlers. Phyllis Notaro was just as popular as any of her male counterparts as one of the program's great champions. Her family ran Angola's Main Bowling Academy, and from there, she became one of the country's top amateur bowlers and a US Open champ in 1961.

The WBEN sports team included Chuck Healy, Dick Rifenburg, Ralph Hubbell, and Don Cunningham.

Early 50s Radio

As Clint Buehlman celebrated 20 years as Buffalo's top morning man in 1952, the team that would be a part of his show for the next 25 years was in place.

Western New Yorkers began waking up to the news of Jack Ogilvie in 1952. He'd been WBEN's evening newscaster and a jack-of-all-

trades at WJTN in Jamestown.

Above: Clint Buehlman, early 1950s.
Left: Jack Ogilvie in WBEN's Statler Hotel Studios, late 1940s.

Buehly's "Mr. Operator," Tom Whalen *(below)* started on the early shift working the Buehlman show in 1948, arriving each day by 4:30 to make sure the studio was ready for Buffalo's AM-MC when his show began at 6am.

Through most of the 1950s, Buehlman's show was Buffalo's most listened to radio program, surpassing even nighttime family shows like Jack Benny, Lux Radio Theater, Fibber McGee & Molly and Dragnet.

During the afternoon hours, WEBR's Bob Wells was most popular, but his ratings didn't even approach Buehlman's.

Right: 1953 ad.

That didn't stop WEBR's owner, The Buffalo Courier-Express, to run stories with headlines like one on 1952 exclaiming "Bob Wells' WEBR Program Rated City's Most Popular," before explaining in the story that the show was "the most popular weekday radio show in Buffalo during the greater part of the afternoon."

BUFFALO'S MOST POPULAR DISC-JOCKEY

Bob Wells
You'll Like What You Hear
And Hear What You Like
2-5:30 P. M.

It's bizarre because it was unnecessary. Even in the moment, Wells was one of the most beloved personalities in the history of Buffalo media as the host of the extraordinarily popular and generation-defining "Hi-Teen" program on WEBR.

Dancers pack the Dellwood Ballroom dance floor for a mid-50's Hi-Teen broadcast.

156

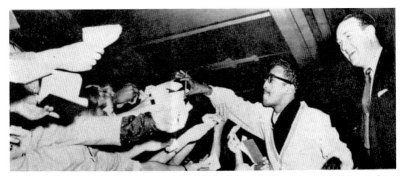

Sammy Davis, Jr. signs autographs while Bob Wells looks on smiling after a performance on the Hi-Teen Show. The program was a known stop for many of the country's top performing artists, who'd gladly give the kids a thrill on a Saturday afternoon before heading to a gig.

Hi-Teen one of Buffalo's most popular radio shows of the era nestled between the end of World War II and the birth of rock 'n' roll.

"I was probably the last disc jockey in America to play an Elvis Presley record," Wells told Ch.2's Rich Kellman during a late 1970s interview.

Toronto's Bluebops on the Hi-Teen stage.

Hi-Teen ran on WEBR for 17 years, hosting as many of 2000 kids in the Dellwood Ballroom at Main and Utica every Saturday.

Wells had been the Assistant Director of Music for Batavia Schools when WEBR General Manager Cy King asked him to produce a live show to help combat juvenile delinquency.

That was January, 1946— and America's record hop was born with the first edition of Wells' show. With the help of the Harold Austin Orchestra keeping the beat, Hi-Teen went on to serve as an inspiration for shows like American Bandstand. The tenth anniversary show, live from The Aud in 1956 attracted 10,000 teens to Memorial Auditorium.

After WEBR, Wells landed at WGR Radio and TV, hosting shows on Ch.2 like Pick-A-Polka, The Yankee Doodle Room (live from AM&A's), and the Money Movie. Even after he was no longer a full-time on-air personality, he could still be seen doing weather on Ch.7's weekend newscasts. He also spent more than 20 years as the radio and television voice of Your Host restaurants.

The stars that Wells missed during the day often wound up on Ed Little's nighttime show on WEBR.

From boy actor to announcer to disc jockey to newsman, Ed Little's 62-year radio career didn't leave much undone.

Discovered by WEBR's Al Zink as an actor in 1938 as a kid actor with a grown-up voice, Ed moved to announcing at WHLD and then WGR in 1942, eventually putting those skills to use for the US Army during World War II.

He'd fly along on bombing missions in the Pacific, recording live descriptions of what he was seeing to be played back over NBC on radios across America.

When he returned home from war, he joined the staff at WBEN, before moving over to WEBR in 1949.

Among other duties there, Ed was the host of a show that broadcast live from the Town Casino, with interviews and interactions with many of the day's biggest stars, who'd stop by the booth to say hello.

In the 60s, he was the newsman on Joey Reynolds' KB Radio show. In the 80s and 90s, his was one of the voices that distinguished WBEN as Buffalo's home for radio news.

Ed's was the last live voice broadcast from the Elmwood Avenue WBEN studios that were the station's home from 1960-2000.

Buffalo lounge piano legend Jackie Jocko appeared regularly on WEBR in the early 1950s along with his partner drummer Joe Peters.

WEBR's "Amanda" interviews an AM&A's buyer on her midday shopping and fashion tips show at the WEBR-970 studios, 23 North Street, in 1951.

"Amanda" was actually Dorothy Shank, president of the local chapter of American Women in Radio & Television. She later worked in marketing for AM&A's, had a show on Ch.4, and was a host on WJJL in Niagara Falls through the 1980s. She was 81 when she died in 1989.

Another piece of Western New York history in the photo: in the middle, between the microphone and the telephone, the 1950's equivalent of a Tim Horton's cup– a glass "to go" coffee cup/milk bottle from Buffalo's ubiquitous Deco Restaurants (there were more than 50 Deco locations around WNY when they were most popular.)

Amanda with Hollywood actress Gloria Swanson.

Warren Michael Kelly, occasionally known as Warren Mike or Warren Kelly, was one of WGR's top on-air talents during his two separate stints there in the 50s.

The Bennett High grad was a newsman at WBNY before serving in the Army during World War II.

After the war, he was Clint Buehlman's newsman at WBEN and spent time in Detroit before coming back to Buffalo to host mornings on WGR. Later, he'd also be seen anchoring newscasts on Ch.2.

He moved on to management and sales, and was General Manager of WYSL and WPHD-FM.

Through the late 40s and early 50s, John Lascalles was WGR's "Man About Midnight." Nicknamed "Ol'Bones," Lascalles would eventually move to mornings on WGR. He was also a familiar face in the early days of Ch.2, as one of the many "Atlantic Weathermen." With the gas station as a sponsor, the man announcing the weather would wear the snappy uniform of an Atlantic gas station attendant while delivering the forecast.

Frank Dill spent a decade at WGR and Ch.2, from the mid-50s through the mid-60s. He was born in Williamsville, but grew up as a sports fanatic near Washington, DC. Like most of his WGR co-workers, Dill was seen and heard in a wide-ranging number of on-air jobs.

On the radio, he was a disc jockey and one of the play-by-play voices of the baseball Bisons. When Ch.2 first signed on, he was a part of the station's original announcing staff as the host of "Sports Corner," the game show "Tune-O," and co-host of "Yankee Doodle" with Bob Wells.

Dill left Buffalo for San Francisco in 1963. When he retired after 34 years there, the paper called him "nice guy Frank Dill -- an oasis of easygoing banter and chuckling good humor."

Jack Mahl   David Getman

Phil Soisson   John Gill

WGR's news men of the 1950s were also widely talented.

Jack Mahl was born in Tonawanda and served in the Army during World War II. He came home to work at WKBW and WGR Radio, eventually spending time at Ch.2 as another of the The Atlantic Weathermen. Through the 70s and 80s, he could be heard up and down Buffalo's radio dial reading news, most notably on WEBR.

David Getman spent a decade as a newsman and Special Events Director for WGR before moving on to public relations roles with the March of Dimes and Buffalo Mayor Chester Kowal.

Phil Soisson came to WGR from WBEN in 1952, and remained a steady news and sports voice on WGR through the 50s and 60s. He was the radio voice of the baseball and hockey Bisons, and anchored news and sports on Ch.2. He was also part of the original Sabres play-by-play team with Ted Darling in 1970.

John Gill started working in radio as an actor in dramas in 1937, and was on the news desk at WGR Radio and then WGR-TV through the 40s, 50s and 60s. He moved to WEBR, where he was one of the main voices of the news-centric 970 format of the late 70s.

Gill was a newsman's newsman. "In 20 years of news reporting for WGR," he said in 1958, "you learn that an analysis of news is vitally important. To paraphrase, every fire isn't a conflagration, nor is every storm a holocaust. It's the highly experienced men on our news staff that accurately describe the news when and as it actually happens."

John Otto would join WGR's news team in the mid '50s, after starting as a newsman and disc jockey at WBNY in 1951. He, by the way, was another Atlantic Weatherman.

Right: Otto stands for a promo shoot on the roof of the Lafayette Hotel.

"Helen Neville possesses one of those rare personalities that sparkles with friendliness and enthusiasm. She has friends and devotees from practically every walk of life."

Neville's broadcasting career began at WGR & WKBW in 1943, and was heard through the 1940s on WKBW's "Modern Kitchen."

Through the 50s, she regularly broadcast on WGR from her home at 1119 Delaware Avenue, interviewing people about the civic and social happenings around Buffalo.

On Ch.2, she hosted "Two For Lunch" (*which later became "Two For Breakfast" when the time slot changed*) for the first six years the station was on the air, 1954-1960.

HELEN NEVILLE

3:45 P.M.
TO
4:00 P.M.

MON. thru FRI.

DIRECT FROM HER HOME—1119 Delaware

Husband & Wife teams

It was vestige of the Vaudeville days—wives and husbands as co-emcees on radio and television, usually hosting otherwise normal shows, only with a special kind of schtick to fall back on.

The successful and beloved team of George Burns and Gracie Allen, the married stars of one of radio's most successful network programs from 1936-50, was all the blueprint local radio programmers needed.

Billy and Reggie Keaton were among the earliest married teams on Buffalo radio starting in the mid-40s, but soon they weren't alone.

When Budd Hulick-- half of the sensational Stoopnagle & Budd comedy team of the 1930s—returned to Western New York radio in the late 40s, he was joined by his wife, Helen. They first appeared on WHLD in her native Niagara Falls, before moving to WKBW for a few years on the "Mr. & Mrs." show. They moved south in the mid-50s, hosting a show on WPTV Ch.5 in Palm Beach starting in 1956.

The Hulicks chat with Lucille Ball & Desi Arnaz on a press trip to Buffalo.

Mary Jane and Seymour Abeles hosted "The Shopper's Guide" on Ch.4.

Both Buffalo natives, Mary Jane was billed as Buffalo's "first and only" female disc jockey during the war years on WGR, and Seymour was a longtime radio actor on all the stations in Buffalo—and received a Bronze star and Purple Heart in the Pacific during World War II.

Bernie and Norma Jean Sandler were well-known for hosting programs showcasing the talents of young people. Future radio stars Danny Neaverth, Tommy Shannon, and Joey Reynolds were all guest teen deejays on Sandler's "The Young Crowd" on WEBR.

Bernie Sandler was a teenaged bandleader while still at Bennett High School, playing gigs at The Colvin Gables and the Glen Casino. After serving in North Africa and Italy during World War II, Sandler moved to radio—first at WBTA in Batavia and then Buffalo's WEBR--where he'd replace Ed Little as the emcee of the Town Casino show in 1953—before moving onto WBEN AM-FM-TV in 1959.

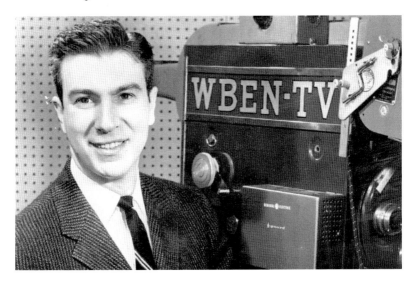

After Bernie had gone to work full-time in marketing for the Iroqouis Brewery and Norma Jane was the director of the Studio Arena School of Theater, the couple hosted "The Sandler Style" on WADV-FM starting in 1969. They were also trusted spokespeople thought the years, often seen together in TV commercials for everything from applesauce to carpets. At the time he died in 1992, Bernie was still on the air weekly at WECK, playing big band music over the radio for the same folks who danced to his live band performances 50 years earlier.

Buffalo's best remembered husband and wife started a 21-year run on Ch.4 on Jan. 17, 1950, with a little cooking, a couple interviews, and a lot of bickering.

"Meet the Millers" with Bill and Mildred Miller was a Buffalo television staple, weekday afternoons for more than two decades.

The program was a melding of the couple's skills. They'd spent more than 20 years entertaining together on the Vaudeville circuit. He was a dancer — even once on Broadway – and she was his piano playing accompanist.

They retired from stage work to Buffalo for health reasons, opening a turkey farm in the Town of Colden—only to answer the call to TV after a handful of very successful cooking segments around Thanksgiving time in 1949.

From the onset, "Meet the Millers" was nominally about "using economy in preparing food," but housewives tuning in around Western New York were just as likely to be entertained by the sometimes-hostile relationship between Bill and Mildred and Mildred's tendency to put Bill in his place regularly. For better or worse, they were Western New York's quintessential quibbling couple.

The show grew to include interview segments which aired Monday, Wednesday and Friday, with cooking segments on Tuesday and Thursday.

The big-name stars who came through Buffalo stayed at the Statler, and that's where Bill and Mildred did their show through the 1950s.

Stars like Elizabeth Taylor and Tony Bennett were guests through the years.

Starting with their first summer on the air, the Millers made bringing Western New York's agricultural fairs to TV viewers a priority.

As the owners of a 350-acre farm, and Bill's role as past president of the state turkey growers' association, the Millers became closely associated especially with the Erie County Fair, from which their show was broadcast live every year.

The Millers were in the inaugural class of the Erie County Fair Hall of Fame in 1989.

After the couple retired from television, Bill was elected Colden supervisor and served through the early 1980s.

The couple moved to Florida, where they passed away in the early 1990s.

Bill and Mildred didn't necessarily cook all the food they showed on TV, and they certainly didn't do the dishes—most of the real kitchen work was done by women like Margaret Teasley, seen here offering some of the shows leftovers to the "Meet the Millers" crew, including Producer Bernie Ross, cameraman Art Lester, floorman Bud Hagmann and studio supervisor Gene Klumpp.

FREQUENCY MODULATION (FM) RADIO STATIONS IN W. N. Y.

Call Letters	Location	Wave Channel	Frequency Megacycles	Kilowatts Power
WBNY-FM	Buffalo	225	92.9	48.3
WJTN-FM	Jamestown	227	93.3	9.5
WHDL-FM	Olean	239	95.7	43
WJJL-FM	Niagara Falls	241	96.1	3
WHEC-FM	Rochester	243	96.5	65
WEBR-FM	Buffalo	245	96.9	9.4
WRNY-FM	Rochester	250	97.9	27
WHLD-FM	Niagara Falls	253	98.5	46
WHFM	Rochester	255	98.9	20
WUSJ-FM	Lockport	257	99.3	0.8
WXRC-FM	Buffalo	277	103.3	4.2
WWOL-FM	Buffalo	281	104.1	13
WBEN-FM	Buffalo	293	106.5	6

"Rising enthusiasm in FM listening throughout Western New York is expected to continue in 1952," started a story in The Buffalo Evening News. Although WBEN first started experimenting with FM on W8XH in 1934, WBEN-FM was Buffalo's first frequency modulation station when it signed on in 1946. Other FM stations signed on the air quickly, and by 1950, there were plenty of choices on the FM dial—although programming was slow to develop for the much clearer sounding band.

It wouldn't be until the late 60s and beyond when many of these still-familiar frequencies would come into their own with programming beyond "whatever was left over" from AM sister stations.

WBEN-FM changed frequencies from 106.5FM to 102.5FM in 1958 so that the station could increase its power.

Accent
on
Variety
10 am to
1:00 am
MUSIC
and news
DIAL 102.5
WBEN-FM

The Four Quarters were regular entertainers on WBEN-TV. Bass player Bassie Atkinson was the only Buffalonian—a Central High grad. Kenneth Strother was on piano; Reggie Willis, guitar; and Eddie Inge, clarinet.

Akron's Miller Bros. Band, shown with Ted Mack as contestants on the Original Amateur Hour, a network program which aired on Ch.4.

Marion Roberts was the hostess of Ch. 4's Plain & Fancy Cooking weekday mornings through much of the 1950s. Her "timely tips make homemaking easier and cooking more exciting," according to a 1955 ad. Ch.4's mid-50s weekday local lineup included Roberts, John Corbett, and Mildred & Bill Miller, all with shows aimed at the housewife.

LOCAL LIGHTS BRIGHTEN YOUR DAYTIME VIEWING on channel **4**

9:30am MARION ROBERTS

PLAIN AND FANCY COOKING
PLAIN AND FANCY TALK
Timely tips every weekday that make home-
making easier . . . and cooking exciting.

1:45pm JOHNNY'S SHOW

His words of money-saving wisdom on new
gimmicks and gadgets brighten your work.
Shopping suggestions Mon.—Wed.—Fri. . .
Tues. and Thurs.—"Speaker of the House."

2:30pm MEET THE MILLERS

Buffalo's favorite TV hosts . . .
with guests, cooking cues, and
comments, Monday through Friday afternoons.

LOCAL SHOWS... **LOCAL** FAVORITES
LOCAL NEWS...THERE'S **MORE** on channel **4**

He came to Buffalo as Ch.4 first signed on— and over the next 30 years, there weren't many radio & TV personalities who saw more airtime than WBEN's John Corbett.

Through the 1950s, he was hosting 11 weekly radio shows and was Ch.4's "Speaker of the House" host weekdays at 12:15pm. Through the 60s and 70s, his duties turned more to news, and in the early 70s, was one of the most seen faces of TV news in Buffalo.

His contract was left to expire in 1977. He was approached

about running for mayor, and even considered it— but ultimately did not, and instead, that election saw James D. Griffin begin his four-term stretch in Buffalo's City Hall.

Celebrating the fifth anniversary of WBEN's Breakfast at the Sheraton with engineer Peter Koelemeyer, organist Nelson Shelby, producer Gene Brook (who also played "Grumbles the Elf" on the Santa show), baritone Harry Schad, and emcees John Corbett and Ed Dinsmore in 1954.

Four years later, John Corbett and Dick Rifenburg celebrate the show's anniversary.

In 1959, the Sheraton Gang included organist Norm Wullen, Dick
Rifenburg, and John Corbett.

By the following year, the Sheraton breakfast show had given way to The
Statler Luncheon Club, in the hotel's Grover Cleveland Room. Virgil
Booth and Mike Mearian were the hosts.

Ed Dinsmore was everywhere on Ch.4 in the station's earliest days, as one of the station's primary newscasters, playing Santa on the Santa show, and host of Breakfast at Sheraton on the radio. Dinsmore might have been Buffalo's most familiar local TV face when he died suddenly in 1954.

Ed Dinsmore (left) and crew get ready for a newscast from the Statler studios of Ch.4, 1954.

Van Miller joined the staff at WBEN-TV as a summer relief announcer in 1955, and didn't leave for 43 years. In this mid-50s shot, Van is anchoring the news while Chuck Healy anchors sports. The pair would play the opposite roles on the same newscast together through much of the following decade.

The first Buffalo scientist to talk meteorology regularly on Buffalo TV was Buffalo Weather Bureau Chief Barney Wiggin.

"Weather with Wiggin" ran Monday evenings in the early 1950s on Ch.4.

Brought to you by...

Two advertisers of the 1950s live on in the memories of Western New Yorkers not only because of the product—but because of the song.

I'm the Jolly Little Baker, and you'll find me on the label, of Kaufman's Rye Bread!

The Kaufman's Bakery stood on Fillmore at Main Street.

Kaufman's Rye Bread's animated little baker danced across Buffalo televisions from the 50s through the 70s. As much as the unique, dense rye bread still sparks life in the palates of Western New Yorkers, our yearning for Kaufman's rye is tied to the fact that the taste is forever linked to that

18-second jingle, permanently implanted in the subconscious of generations of Buffalonians-- which many of us could still sing on demand.

Then there's the address that many of us know even though we never stepped foot in the store which closed in 1982.

Shop and save at Sattler's... 9-9-8 Broad-WAY!

While the (in)famous jingle indeed helped Buffalo remember that now iconic address, more than that, without the jingle-- we might not have known Sattler's at all.

Despite decades of heavy print advertising and growing from a single store front to an entire block across from the Broadway Market, Sattler's couldn't seem to bust through as much more than a neighborhood Broadway/Fillmore store.

It was the first-ever advertising jingle created for a department store, written by New York City's "Singing Sweethearts" Lanny and Ginger Grey in 1941. There were different versions, but they all ended in those five syllables that are permanently etched into the memories of generations of Buffalonians, "nine-nine-eight Broad-WAY!"

The radio singing commercials did something that years of print ads just couldn't do. People from all over Buffalo, especially more elusive wealthy customers, started shopping 998, where they were buying everything from canaries to thuringer sausage to mink coats at Sattler's.

In 1948, the Sattler's store was completely rebuilt, complete with escalators and air conditioning. Sattler's executives called called it "the store that jingles built."

Those iconic jingles filled Buffalo's airwaves in 1950, playing 102 times a week on WBEN, WGR, WKBW, WEBR and WBNY.

Sattler's was at the forefront of over-the-top, cutting-edge marketing and self-promotion.

It was nearly impossible to listen to the radio for any extended period of time without being reminded to "shop and save at Sattler's, 998 Broadway!"

The original Sattler's, 998 Broadway across from the Broadway Market. Sattler's closed in 1982, and the building was torn down to make way for a Kmart store in the late 80s. In 2012, an Aldi supermarket opened at the fabled address.

Buffalo's Forgotten TV Pioneers: WBES-TV & WBUF-TV

For five years, WBEN-TV Ch.4 was Buffalo's only television station.

Then in 1953, two more stations came to the market—but most Buffalonians needed special equipment to watch them.

Buffalo's WBUF-TV Ch.17 and WBES-TV Ch.59 took advantage of the federal government opening up a much wider spectrum of television broadcasting frequencies. *Ultra High Frequency* or UHF channels 14-83 were opened up in 1952.

Up until then, televisions were built only with VHF receivers, and could only pick up channels 2-13.

Encouraging sales of special converter boxes was only part of the uphill battle for WBUF-TV and WBES-TV.

Sales of new televisions and converter boxes skyrocketed in 1953.

VHF stations 2-13 offered much better reception, and there were a number of interested parties in Buffalo petitioning to become the license holders for stations on Ch. 2 and Ch.7, which allotted to Buffalo, but not yet assigned to licensees.

As those cases were being made in Washington, two local investment groups rolled the dice on UHF here-- but those two groups had entirely different stomachs for gambling.

WBUF-TV was founded by a couple of friends looking to strike out on their own.

Sherwin Grossman was a 28-year old Lafayette High

and UB grad working in his family dry cleaning plant and Gary Cohen was managing his family's movie theater business at Tonawanda's Sheridan Drive-In. (That family business is now run by Rick Cohen at Lockport's Transit Drive-In).

The pair first set sights on bringing television to Jamestown—until an investor convinced them to aim for a bigger market just to the northwest.

On December 18, 1952, the FCC granted them the construction permit for WBUF-TV, Ch.17 in Buffalo.

Further up the dial, the group that founded WBES-TV had much more on the line, both reputationally and financially.

Western Savings Bank President Charles Diebold, Davis Heating & Refrigerating President Joseph Davis, and attorney Vincent Gaughan were the leadership team who were granted an FCC permit for WBES-TV, Ch.59 in Buffalo, five days after WBUF-TV on December 23, 1952.

In less than a week, Buffalo went from a one-station market to what promised to be a three-station market.

Up until the time that new stations signed-on, Ch.4 was in the catbird's seat—having the prime pick of programming from the CBS, NBC, ABC, and DuMont television networks.

"We're shuffling back to Buffalo"

"Toast of the Town" returns to your TV screen through the facilities of WBUF-TV

Ed Sullivan's Sunday night staple— known as "Toast of the Town" before it was renamed "the Ed Sullivan Show" in 1955-- was one of many nationally popular shows which Ch.4 chose not to air. In the time just before WBUF-TV signed on, Ch.4 was running game show "the Big Payoff" during the Ed Sullivan time slot.

Ch.4's owners, The Buffalo Evening News, covered developments at WBUF and WBES with the paper's usual reserve. But over at the Courier-Express, daily blow-by-blow developments were compared and contrasted, and it was made into a race to which station might go on the air first.

"Buffalo's two new UHF stations open a hopeful new chapter in the Western New York television story," reported the Courier-Express as both stations were poised to begin broadcasting. "UHF means considerably more free home entertainment, and a delightfully specific opportunity to turn the dial."

WBUF-TV purchased 184 Barton Street—later the home of WGR-TV and then WNED-TV-- dubbing it "Television City." There, they built and equipped a full television studio complex.

When the station first signed on, WBUF-TV's mascot was Buffalo Bill.

WBES-TV moved into the penthouse at the Lafayette Hotel, and built a tower on the roof—which at the time, was Buffalo's tallest structure. The lower portion of that tower still stands on the building today. The space inside the station was limited—but included offices, a small studio, and the station's transmitter plant. There were also promises to put the hotel's ballroom to use as the home of a huge, audience participation kids show.

"We think we have found the three keys to ultimate success and public acceptance," Gaughan, the father of Buffalo attorney and regionalism proponent Kevin Gaughan, announced. "They are power, personnel, and programming. With these assets, WBES-TV can offer the people of Western New York the very best in television."

Ch.59 made splashy hires of known and beloved Buffalo personalities. Roger Baker, who was still occasionally announcing sports, was also WKBW's General Manager when WBES-TV hired him to run the new station and to be the station's newscaster. Woody Magnuson, longtime WBEN announcer and children's host, was hired to become the station's program director.

"Life begins at 59" was the headline sprawled across a full-page ad in the Courier-Express. "The best in television… a great range of fine programs to delight and interest your entire family (through) the miracle of UHF."

WBUF's staff hires weren't quite as newsworthy, but they also had a full-page ad that was just as over-the-top, billing themselves as "the modern miracle that gives you what you want — when you want it — in your own home" and "solace and comfort, laughter and joy, tears and sighs, company in loneliness and solitude in crowds, escape and challenge, fact and fiction… Aladdin and his wonderful lamp, Alice and her miraculous mirror, Jack the Giant Killer, Paul Bunyan the Great American."

It was WBUF-TV Ch.17 that made it on the air first by a month, with a schedule of mostly network programming starting August 17, 1953. WBES-TV Ch.59 signed on September 23, 1953.

In the WBUF-TV control room, with coffee from Your Host restaurants.

Ch.59, however, fell out of the gate. Technical problems delayed the station's signing on, and sponsors were slow to sign up. WBUF-TV had many of the same issues, but WBES-TV's investors soured immediately to the station's hemorrhaging of money, and on December 18, 1953—less than a year after being awarded the station and 13 weeks after signing on— WBES-TV, Ch.59 returned its license to the federal government.

Being alone as "Buffalo's other TV station" helped Ch.17 a bit, but it, too was losing money. The station's saving grace came in the form of the

National Broadcasting Company, trying to outfox the federal government's limit on the number of VHF stations that a television network could own.

Jack Begon was an NBC foreign correspondent who was brought to Buffalo as a news anchor on WBUF. He spent much of his career stationed in Rome for NBC and later ABC.

WRESTLING
from
BUFFALO

MEMORIAL
AUDITORIUM

WBUF

CHANNEL 17

In 1956, after WBES-TV signed off and WGR-TV Ch.2 had already signed on, NBC bought WBUF-TV as an experiment to see whether the network would be able to build a UHF station which rose to the standards of its other VHF properties.

NBC built a state-of-the-art television facility at 2077 Elmwood Avenue, and brought in network-level talent from around the country to staff local programs.

Like Ch.4, Ch.17 also carried live wrestling from the Aud.

TOMORROW

OCTOBER 11, 1956

WBUF • CHANNEL 17

WILL BE FORMALLY DEDICATED BY DAVE GARROWAY AND NBC OFFICIALS. THE CEREMONIES WILL ORIGINATE FROM OUR NEW STUDIOS AT 2077 ELMWOOD AVENUE ON "TODAY". WE ARE GRATEFUL FOR THE WARM WELCOME WE HAVE RECEIVED FROM OUR NEW NEIGHBORS OF THE NIAGARA FRONTIER AND PLEDGE OURSELVES TO EVEN GREATER SERVICE TO THIS, OUR COMMUNITY. IT IS WITH GREAT PRIDE THAT WE BRING TO YOU, OUR FRIENDS AND NEIGHBORS, THE FINEST IN TELEVISION ENTERTAINMENT, FEATURING THAT GREAT ARRAY OF NBC NETWORK PROGRAMS AND STARS, PLUS AN IMPRESSIVE LINE-UP OF NEW AND DIFFERENT LOCAL SHOWS.

The Today Show broadcast live from WBUF's new 2077 Elmwood studios, shown here. Less than four years later, the building would be home to WBEN and Ch.4.

After two years, the network called the experiment a bust, with the station still losing money and Buffalo's ratings on network shows lagging well behind the network averages.

WBUF-TV's Mac McGarry gives a weather report, 1957. McGarry covered President Truman's inauguration for NBC in 1948. After leaving Buffalo, he returned to Washington, and anchored NBC News updates through the 70s and 80s. He also hosted the Washington DC version of "It's Academic" on NBC-owned station WRC-TV for 50 years.

WBUF-TV went dark on October 1, 1958. NBC donated the license to the group that formed Buffalo's educational public TV broadcaster, WNED-TV.

With public broadcasting on Ch.17, Buffalo would be without a commercial UHF station until WUTV Ch.29 signed on in 1970.

*Frank Frederics was the only on-air personality who was seen regularly
through most of WBUF-TV's tumultuous history. He was the News
Director when the station signed on, and was the only original announcer
retained when NBC bought the station. During the NBC years, he
anchored a newscast sponsored by Milk For Health. Live commercials
during the newscast were hosted by Jan Okun— who later spent more than
40 years as the Food Editor at The Buffalo News.*

It's not the end of the story, though. Even if we don't remember their call
letters, the legacy of Buffalo's UHF pioneers lives on.

Ch.17 operates as a public service in Buffalo to this day.

The studios built by Ch.59 at the Lafayette were the first home of Ch.2 and
then the home of WNED-TV.

WBUF-TV's Barton Street studios were the second home of Ch.2, and in a
familiar pattern, became the home of WNED and Western New York
Public Broadcasting when WGR-TV moved to Delaware Avenue.

And the Elmwood Avenue studios built by NBC have been the home of
Ch.4 since 1960.

Rick Azar was WBUF-TV's Atlantic Weatherman.

Both stations also served as the dial spot where a handful of later well-known Buffalo television personalities got their first chance in front of the camera, most notably, WBES-TV's 20-year-old staff announcer Tom Jolls (right) and WBUF-TV's sports reporter and "Weathervane" host, Rick Azar.

And at least one local star of Buffalo's early UHF stations has been seen on local TVs over the last several years. Doris Jones—who was Doris Sherris as your "Phoenix (Beer) All Weather Gal" on WBES-TV continues to help on pledge drives on WNED-TV.

Buffalo's Willis Conover

Willis Conover with Louis Armstrong, in the VOA studios in Washington.

When Benny Goodman wanted to quote a jazz expert, Willis Conover was the man he quoted. In 1960, The Courier-Express called the Kenmore High alum Conover "the most popular disc jockey in the world." But even then, no one in Buffalo—or even the USA—had heard of him.

With 30 million people listening to his program every day, Conover was the definitive voice of American Jazz all around the world on The Voice of America-- a federal-government operated series of shortwave radio stations beamed everywhere but our part of North America.

Through the years, his hometown had quick tastes of Conover's abilities-- like a series produced by John Hunt on WBFO in 1980, showcasing the man and the music he loved.

But mostly, the kid from Villa Avenue who attended Bennett and Kenmore High Schools and became the man described by President Carter as "devoted... to the story of American music" and called "the world's most popular American" has gone mostly forgotten in the city he considered home.

The Rico Family

Conover might have been the world's favorite jazz disc jockey, but in 1950's Buffalo, Joe Rico was tops.

He started spinning what Buffalo Evening News radio reporter Ray Finch called "smoking hot discs" in 1947 on WWOL Radio, before moving to WEBR in the mid-50s, WUFO, and then WADV-FM through the 70s.

A steady, smooth deep-throated delivery and a knowledge of and love for jazz made Rico "the epitome of cool," according to critic Gary Deeb.

EVERYTHING'S "COOL" AT MUSIC HOUSE

LISTEN TO . . .

"JUMP for JOE"

WITH JOE RICO

NIGHTLY 6 to 8:30

1120 on Your DIAL

WWOL

Sponsored by

Music House

Jazz Record Centers

JOE RICO—YOUR GOOD NEIGHBOR

JOE PRESENTS RENDEZVOUS at 6:30 P.M. FOR WEEK NIGHTS. LATER DINNERTIME RELAXATION. IT'S JAZZ CENTRAL at 11:30 P.M. BOTH ARE FINE LISTENING.

WEBR · 970

970 KC ★ 5000 WATTS ★ 970 KC ★ 5000 WATTS

Rico's influence mattered to the musicians of the jazz world. Stan Kenton's "Jump for Joe" was named with Rico in mind, as was Count Basie's "Port o' Rico."

As much as he was known for bringing jazz to Buffalo's radio dials, he was just as involved in bringing the top musicians in the country to perform in Buffalo.

As a promoter, Joe Rico's greatest triumph was the Buffalo Jazz Festival—
a nearly impossible to imagine lineup over two days at Offermann Stadium
in 1960.

Joe Rico was raised in radio. His parents were the heart and the voice of Buffalo's Italian-American community. For 50 years, Emelino Rico — known to listeners of "Neapolitan Serenade" as "Papa Rico" and the head of "Casa Rico" — broadcast Italian music, in Italian, for Italians, from his home on Seventh Street on Buffalo's Italian West Side.

For most of five decades, come 10:30am, the Liberty Bell March would open another program of cultural pride, personal warmth and a taste of the old country. While he was heard on many stations through the years, often two or three stations at the same time, for 45 years the Ricos were heard on WHLD 1270AM.

Emelino came to America as a movie producer in 1922. Ten years later, on a stop in Buffalo, he met Mary Pinieri, who was destined to become the West Side's beloved Mama Rico.

Mama Rico told listeners to their 50th anniversary celebration on WHLD in 1985 that their lives were spent highlighting the best in Italian music and culture, "helping others, and doing charitable work."

The Ricos worked to bring some of Italy to Buffalo, and some of Buffalo to Italy, with many trips and exchanges. Papa liked to tell the story of a

1967 audience with Pope Paul VI, when His Holiness greeted him immediately by saying, "You run the Italian program in Buffalo."

Many of Buffalo's most famous Italian-Americans said the time spent at Casa Rico helped jump start their career -- folks like Tony Award-winning choreographer Michael Bennett and pianist Leonard Pennario.

Like many other immigrant Rust Belt cities, foreign language broadcasts were very popular in Buffalo. Matt Korpanty spent more than 40 years broadcasting in Polish, primarily on WHLD, starting in 1940. His Polish language show was produced from his private studio in the heart of Polonia at 761 Fillmore Avenue.

Buffalo's Polka King

As the 1950s wore on, Stan "Stas" Jasinski would become known as Buffalo's Polka King with his daily programs first heard on WWOL and WXRA, and then on powerful WKBW. The platform and his mix of Polish and English songs and commercials gave him a voice heard by the Greater Buffalo community as well as Polish-Americans.

Jasinski went on to found WMMJ Radio, which became WXRL when he sold the station to the Schriver Family as he began plans to sign-on WUTV Ch.29. Jasinski eventually sold Ch.29 as well, but continued playing polkas on the radio for a total of 60 years when he retired in 2000.

Buffalo's Last Staff Organist

His lasting fame might be as the Memorial Auditorium organist for the Sabres and the Braves, but that was Norm Wullen's retirement job-- after spending decades as one of Buffalo's highest profile radio and TV organ and piano men.

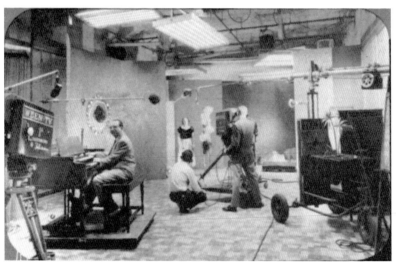

Norm Wullen plays as the show goes on, on Ch.4

He grew up on Buffalo's East Side as the son of a piano tuner. His music career started just after World War I at the age of 15, behind a drum kit on the Crystal Beach boat. He soon moved on to piano, playing over the silent movies at the old Shea's Court Street Theater. From there, he could be heard as the organ backdrop for the vaudeville circuit at the 20th Century and Shea's Hippodrome theaters, appearing through the years with Bob Hope, Frank Sinatra, George Burns, Jack Benny and Edgar Bergen.

Teamed with his brother Charley, he gained his first radio plaudits on WBEN in 1934. "The Wullen Brothers" act was a dueling piano team.

Norm replaced Bobby Nicholson as WBEN's staff organist in the 1940s, and was constantly heard on WBEN and seen on Ch.4. On TV, he accompanied Rollie Huff, and later Dick Rifenburg, as they did their morning exercises.

On the radio he was a fixture on the live midday "breakfast" shows that broadcast live from the restaurants and tea rooms of department stores and hotels like the Yankee Doodle Room at AM&A's, the Turf Room at the Sheraton, and the Grover Cleveland Room at the Statler.

Dick Rifenburg, John Corbett, & Norm Wullen

By the end of the 1950s, Norm and staff musicians at all the local radio and TV stations were being squeezed out by a change in musical taste, but while he was still playing, Wullen took his task of "setting the mood" for housewives during their morning coffee break very seriously.

"I deplore rock 'n' roll," said Wullen in 1957, "not because it's riding a crest of popularity, but because it lacks any real melody."

The News called Wullen "the flower of WBEN's Musical world," even as Top 40 began to take a strangle hold of Buffalo radio.

"Radio listeners dialing about in search of good music these weekday mornings have been finding their quest satisfied by nothing more tried-and-true than harmonious organ music," said Wullen.

Even as times changed, Wullen and crew evolved. A little, anyway.

Like the time in 1962, toward the end of the Breakfast Show's run that host John Corbett called out for "a little Twist music."

Wullen was ready. It wasn't Chubby Checker, but Norm's musical meanderings fit the bill, "bouncing out pleasant notes," if not a Twist.

Along with fellow radio pioneer Elvera Ruppel, Norm Wullen was also a Buffalo television pioneer, playing piano and accompanying the soprano on the "Miss Melody" show, Thursdays through the late 40s and early 50s on WBEN-TV.

Elvera Ruppel and Norm Wullen on Ch.4 in the early 1950s.

Ruppel sang at Shea's Buffalo with the BPO, with those concerts frequently sent out around the country on the various radio networks. She was a regular star of the musical programs with pianist Al Erisman on WMAK Radio through the 1920s, and as a favorite of WGR musical director David Cheskin, her voice was heard frequently on Buffalo radio through the 30s and 40s as well.

Her most critically acclaimed moments in the spotlight came when she was half of "Buffalo's Radio Sweetheart" team, as partnered with Smiling Bob Smith—later of Howdy Doody fame—on WGR.

For the Kiddos on Ch.4

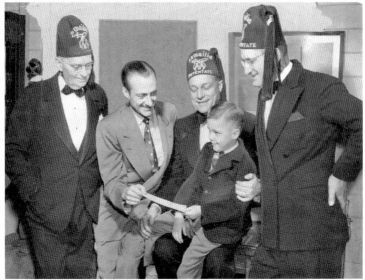

In the early days on Ch.4, Woody Magnuson brought his popular "Uncle Ben" character from radio to TV. Here, he helps Shriners reward the boy who won a contest to name the zoo's new gnu in 1950.

Ch.4's Uncle Jerry & pianist Aunt Annie Fadale on "Uncle Jerry's Club."

Uncle Jerry's Club started on Channel 4 in 1955, and ran on Sunday morning through the rest of the decade. Jerry Brick was the floor director of "Meet the Millers" during the week, but on Sunday, he filled the Statler Hotel Ballroom with kids ready to show their talents in exchange for prizes like Parker Brothers board games and tickets to the latest Disney films.

Becoming Uncle Jerry's next star was easy. "He holds open house every Thursday, at 4 in the WBEN studios in Hotel Statler. Jerry's booming voice and winning smile —emanating from a 6-2 243-pound frame—welcome all youngsters, age 6-14."

From 1958 to 1974, husband
and wife puppeteers Bob and
Ellen Knechtel brought
whimsy and fantasy to Ch.4's
kids shows with marionettes
and puppets they'd create
and perform with. The sets
for shows like "Storybook
Land" and "Puppet
Carnival" were built and
designed by Ch.4's talented
artist Ted Patton, who also
built sets for Meet the Millers
and the Santa show.

The Knechtels' most famous creation was Uncle Mike's sidekick Buttons.

One of WBEN's most versatile and high-profile talents, Mike Mearian came to the Evening News Stations from WKBW in 1952.

An Army boxing champ and multiple Purple Heart winner during World War II, Mearian was a talented and imaginative writer and actor in both radio and television, and a warm friendly personality on the housewives-focused Luncheon programs he hosted with Virgil Booth on WBEN.

The announcer and program host is best remembered for his role as "Uncle Mike" (and later Captain Mike) on Children's Theater, which started on Ch. 4 in 1952.

Buttons was Uncle Mike's constant companion on those shows— the puppet was created by Ch.4's puppetmasters Bob and Ellen Knechtel specifically for Mearian and the type of show he wanted to produce.

When he left WBEN for acting roles in New York City, some were concerned that kids might get the wrong idea about "Uncle Mike's" first big acting gig: The spokesman for Tareyton Cigarettes. He had steady work through the 90s, when he was cast several times as a judge on "Law & Order."

Through the years, the sets—and therefore the names—changed on Mike Mearian's Children's Theater. When Popeye cartoons became part of the show, he became "Captain Mike" with "Buttons the Cabin Boy." The final set for the show before Mearian left Ch.4 was in "Uncle Mike's attic."

Before WBEN Program Director Bill Peters would become known to a generation of kids as "the real" Santa Claus on Ch.4, he hosted cartoons as Little Wally on Sunday mornings. Peters also frequently appeared with Van Miller's radio show as "Norman Oklahoma."

Like every other member of the WBEN announcer staff, Virgil Booth just about did it all on Ch.4 and the AM and FM radio stations, from disc jockey to TV and radio newscasts from the time he joined the station in 1950.

With Mike Mearian, Booth was the announcer on the long-running line of midday shows for housewives that were broadcast live from hotel restaurants and department store tea rooms.

News TV critic J. Don Schlaerth called him "a cheerful broadcaster with a reserved manner." That, along with his background as an English teacher, made him the perfect man to become the host of "Fun to Learn" and programs with Clayton Freiheit at Buffalo Zoo and Ellsworth Jaeger at the Buffalo Museum of Science starting in 1951.

He had his turn at hosting kids cartoon programs, too, as "the baggage master" on "The Big Mac Show" and "Mischief Makers," and then in the title role on the afternoon program "Mr. Bumble's Curiosity Shop."

Aside from Casper the Friendly Ghost cartoons—which were beckoned by Mr. Bumble's ringing of an invisible bell, Booth would also narrate old silent-film era Our Gang shorts and other more educational short films as well.

Mr. Bumbles takes about 30 minutes putting on makeup and costume each Saturday afternoon," reported The Buffalo Evening News in a profile. "He becomes a man in his 70s who uses the language of children to heighten their inquisitiveness during the 5 to 6 PM Saturday program."

Virgil Booth was WBEN's Mr. Science, the soft-spoken and gentle soul who educated children while entertaining them on shows like "Your Museum of Science."

"Fun to Learn" was an educational show that dated back to the earliest days on Ch.4. Buffalo State's Dr. Howard Conant was one of the hosts of the show when the focus was art.

Grumbles the Elf, Santa, and the unforgettable Forgetful the Elf.

From 1948 to 1973, the children of Buffalo knew who the one, true Santa was — and it was the guy who read their letters on Ch.4.

During most of the 25 years the show aired, Hengerer's sponsored the show to run from Thanksgiving to Christmas Eve for 15 minutes on weekdays, a little longer on Saturdays. In 1956, the show that delivered approximately 50,000 letters to Santa through its run became Buffalo's first locally-produced show regularly presented in color.

Ed Dinsmore as Santa, with Grumbles, Freezy, and Mrs. Claus.

Two different men played Santa on Channel 4. Announcer Ed Dinsmore was the first St. Nick from the show's inception until his death in 1954.

Station program director Bill Peters — who was also known on the Van Miller Show as Norman Oklahoma — played Santa from 1954 until the program ended with his death 19 years later.

Santa, however, was barely the star of the show.

Forgetful the Elf, played memorably by WBEN copy writer and librarian John Eisenberger, was there for the entire run of the show from 1948-73.

Not only was the elf he played forgetful, but he was silly. Most shows revolved around Forgetful trying to paint Santa's sleigh with polka dots, or trying to convince Santa to get rid of his "old fashioned" red suit for something a bit more modern.

Forgetful helps Santa (being played by Bill Peters) map out his route for Christmas Eve.

Hundreds of times through the show's quarter century, Forgetful was seen greasing up the reindeer's antlers, with the hopes of making them go faster.

The show's theme song was Leroy Anderson's "Sleigh Ride," which was also frequently used during the Christmas season by WBEN's legendary morning man Clint Buehlman.

No full episodes or even short clips of this show — which ran for 25 years — are known to exist. The show was usually presented live, and recording was a more costly and difficult endeavor than it is today.

Santa and Forgetful had plenty of helpers through the years, all of whom — just like Peters and Eisenberger — had other jobs around the station.

Grumbles the Elf was played by executive director Gene Brook and then floor manager Bud Hagman. Another director, Warren Jacober, played Freezy the Polar Bear. There were countless other puppets and guest stars, but none rising even close to the popularity of Eisenberger's Forgetful.

The show ended when Bill Peters died in 1973. Eisenberger died in 1984 at the age of 72.

John Eisenberger was truly a man of many talents. From his time as one of Smilin' Bob Smith's "High Hat Trio," to acting on Broadway, to his time on WBEN playing country music as "Old Saddlebags," Forgetful was only the tip of the iceberg.

Beginnings of a Teenage Revolution: The Hound, Lucky Pierre, & Hernando

The Hound Dog made a permanent mark on the pop culture history of America with his nightly show on WKBW from 1954-58. Starting in the late 40s, George Lorenz was known as "the Ol'man," "Ol'Dad Lorenz," and "Daddy Dog" before "The Hound Dog" stuck as a nickname.

Known for his *hep* records and jive talk, he refused to give the time and temperature on the air. When he did commercials for Mother Goldstein's wine, he'd sample it on the air.

After spending time at a few smaller stations, in the mid-50s, The Hound took his rhythm and blues program-- featuring the music which would soon be known as rock 'n' roll-- to 50,000-watt WKBW Radio.

The powerful signal allowed "The Hound" to introduce the evolving music genre to the entire northeastern United States. "The Hound" was the Godfather of rock 'n' roll radio, not just in Buffalo but around the country.

The Hound with Bill Haley and His Comets.

217

As a teenager working at a gas station, his first radio job came as an actor in dramas in the late 1930s. He got the job "because of his ability in imitating various dialects," the Courier-Express reported, adding that he'd "often been cast in the role of the slicker in the racketbusting plays."

A decade later, he was doing his Hound Dog routine on Niagara Falls' WJJL. By the mid 50's, Lorenz's hip daddy style, and the fact that he was spinning soulful records from the original black artists — not the sanitized crooner re-sings heard elsewhere on the radio — made him an institution.

An unlikely hero of Buffalo teenagers, "The Hound" made it about the music and bringing rhythm and blues to a wider audience. It went beyond the records. Events promoted by Lorenz usually included black and white artists playing together at a time in the mid-50s when that wasn't always the case. Those audiences were also mixed racially.

A Hound Dog record hop at the Hadji Temple, 118 E. Utica Street, with both black and white teens in attendance. The Hound's secretary, Betty Shampoe, is to the left on the stage. This photo is from her collection.

When his voice came through the speaker on your radio, you knew you were hearing something you weren't going to hear anywhere else. He was rock 'n' roll even before the phrase rock 'n' roll existed.

Ironically, the man who introduced Elvis at Memorial Auditorium was out at KB when the station went rock 'n' roll full-time in 1958. Lorenz wanted nothing to do with a Top-40 format, and was known to give the time and temperature at the beginning of his show, and told listeners to "set their clocks and thermometers, because that was the last time they were going to hear that for the next four hours."

Elvis Presley and George "Hound Dog" Lorenz, Memorial Auditorium.

While inspiring many of the changes that came to KB and many other stations around the country, the Hound stayed true to his style and founded WBLK Radio, where he continued to uncover and spotlight new rhythm and blues artists in Buffalo and to a syndicated audience around the country.

Hernando's Hideaway hit Buffalo radios in 1954 from the studios of WXRA, which was licensed to Kenmore, but broadcast from studios on Niagara Falls Boulevard, in a spot that was later the long-time home of Swiss Chalet (and today is a vacant lot in front of Outback Steakhouse.)

With a Spanish accent, it was Phil Todaro behind what The Buffalo Evening News called "Hernando's delightfully fanciful nonsense."

His show ran evenings every day but Saturday, and from the rhythm and blues music he played, to outings at Crystal Beach and serving bottles of Canada Dry and Oscar pop at his remote broadcasts, the program was clearly geared to the burgeoning teen demographic.

After making offerings on the air, Hernando received more than 3000 mailed requests in two weeks for his "Slang Slogans" dictionary of teen-age vernacular.

The one day he was off in the evening, "Hernando on Campus" was heard Saturday mornings, where "the popular DJ spotlights top tunes determined by survey of the local high schools and colleges and includes a calendar of their upcoming social events."

He eventually made his way to evenings on WGR Radio before leaving radio for music full time. Among his musical offerings most memorable to Western New Yorkers came as co-writer of *Wild Weekend* with Tom Shannon. The *Rockin' Rebels* hit was an instrumental version Shannon's radio theme song.

Lucky Pierre, the back of this card says, was born in Paris in 1934, and goes on to say his "rapid rise to popularity, accomplished in the few short years since his arrival in Buffalo, is a result of his rare combination of old-world charm and modern effervescence. His refreshingly different qualities have captured the imaginations of young and old alike."

After coming to Western New York radio in 1954 at WWOL, where he was not only a disc jockey—but as an amateur boxer and semi-pro football player was named sports director as well.

He moved on to WHLD briefly before heading to WEBR in 1955, and then WBNY before leaving town for Los Angeles, where he'd spent most of the next 60 years on the radio and pioneering the disco and dancing format in the market, as well as hosting a TV cooking show for housewives in the early 60s.

His most adoring fans were the girls and women who were spellbound by his accent and accompanying smooth style.

"Though he's not very handsome, and he's not very strong… in a cabin in the blizzard he's the one you bring along!" chanted his opening song on

WBNY, which continued, "I'm the man of the hour, I'm the man of the year… I'm the man that every living husband has the right to fear…. I'm Lucky Pierre!!"

1955 ad shows Lucky Pierre and a young Rick Azar before he headed to WBUF-TV. Nan Cooper spent more than two decades offering household tips on WBEN, including for the full run of "Newsday at Noon," 1978-96.

Legacy of the Seneca-Babcock Boys' Club

For many kids and teens of the Eisenhower era, the different kinds of sounds coming out of radios gave them something of their own to listen to while doing their homework or on a transistor radio snuck under a pillow after bedtime.

There are also those who listened to deejays like The Hound and Lucky Pierre and were inspired to spend the next 60 years entertaining the world.

For example, Buffalo radio legends Sandy Beach and Jefferson Kaye, both of whom grew up in Massachusetts, listened to the Hound over KB's powerful signal as youngsters and cited him as an inspiration.

But right here in Buffalo, a handful of the boys who'd be the broadcast Pied Pipers of their generation got their radio start in an old brick building in South Buffalo's Seneca-Babcock neighborhood.

A group of friends from St. Monica's grammar school on Orlando Street spent most of the rest of their free time at the Boys' Club a couple blocks away on Babcock Street.

The club's organized activities, mostly sports, weren't exactly what these boys were after. "They weren't much for boxing," activities director Jimmy Coyle would say for years after, "they were more for talking."

Dan Neaverth   Bill Masters   Joey Reynolds   Dan McBride

Four Buffalo announcer-disc jockeys are Boys' Club alumni

Past members of the Babcock Boys' Club, from the Courier-Express, 1964

Danny Neaverth, Joe Pinto (who'd later become Joey Reynolds on the radio), Bill Masters (who spent 20 years on WEBR and WBEN), Danny McBride (whose local broadcasting career spanned 60 years) were all major players starting a closed-circuit radio station for the club.

Joey Pinto, center, brought his home record player to the Boys' Club when the one in the club broke. That's Joe Marszalak and Richard Quinn with him in a photo that ran in the Buffalo Evening News in 1956.

The boys convinced Boys' Club manager Gurney Jenkins to get rid of an old jukebox that played 78 rpm records for Monday night dances and replace it with a modern record player and a microphone. Once they got the green light, all the boys went to work.

WBCB could only be heard inside the Babcock Boys' Club, but offered Buffalo the first taste of what would fill the airwaves for decades to come.

Joe Pinto sent letters to record promoters and radio stations asking for old, about to be discarded, or greatly discounted records. He walked all over the city to collect the 45s which offered a more modern beat for the Boys' Club dances.

Neaverth and McBride wired the whole building for sound, and now the set-up was more than just for dances in the gym. There was music, news, and even commercials on a regular schedule. They boys eventually started doing play-by-play of the sporting events at the club.

And a decade before their KB Radio cross-talk between Neaverth's afternoon show and Reynolds' evening show became the talk of Buffalo, the same two kids became the talk of South Buffalo with their "pretend" radio station at the Boys' Club.

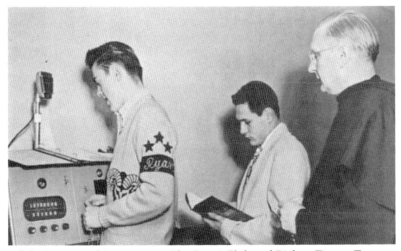

While Danny and Joey were at The Boys' Club and Bishop Timon, Tom Shannon was at Bishop Ryan High, getting one of his first on air gigs leading the school in the rosary as Fr. Rufus looked on.

Boys' Club veteran Danny McBride serves Pepsi-Cola and hot dogs at a WEBR Record Hop.

WEBR deejays Tap Taplin, Bob Wells, Bernie Sandler, and Jack Eno prepare to broadcast live for a full week from the newest Your Host restaurant in the Sheridan Drive Plaza, Sheridan at Niagara Falls Blvd. in 1953.

WKBW's ultra-modern Radio Center was actually a refaced barn which stood next door to the Churchill Tabernacle building. It was built out in 1951 in the parking lot of Tabernacle—which by the end of the decade was destined to become the home of WKBW-TV Ch.7.

"The Calm Before the Storm"

As songs like "Rock Around The Clock" by Bill Haley & His Comets hit number one on the charts, Elvis Presley was still receiving second billing to Slim Whitman and Andy Griffith in stage shows around the south.

"Rhythm and blues" was still working its way into "rock 'n' roll," and it was still a little time before Elvis started to become recognized first as "the hottest hillbilly attraction" and "the king of western bop."

Young people were paying attention, but society— not yet.

Even though The Hound was on KB in 1955, his sound was not reflective of the station by any means.

In fact, The Hound's lead-in show six nights a week was Stan Jasinski's Polka Beehive.

Friday, September 14, 1956

FRIDAY NIGHT'S RADIO

Stations Frequently Change Programs Without Notice. Color T

WBEN 930 CBS*	WEBR 970 MBS*	WKBW 1520	WGR 550 ABC*	WBNY 1400
6:00 News, weather	News; Wall St.	News	News	Songs by
6:15 Sport, Hubbell	Bailey, sports	Sports Extra	Mrizer, sports	Crosby
6:30 Mike Mearian	Accordionist	Polka Bee-	Music, o'doors	News
6:45 Low Thomas*	Paul & Ford	hive, Stan	Newsbeat	Wings Song
7:00 Amos 'n' Andy	Fulton Lewis*	Jasinski	E. P. Morgan*	Bob
7:15 Music Hall*	Welk's Orch.	The Hound	Mel Allen*	and
7:30 Bing Crosby*	Gab. Heatter*	Dog	Mystery time	Ray
7:45 Edw. Murrow*	Golf	Show	News	News

The programs and talent that WKBW Radio was promoting in 1956-- only a matter of months before rock 'n' roll Top 40 would change radio forever-- looks much more like KB did in 1930 than it would in 1960.

WKBW INC.
BUFFALO, NEW YORK

WKBW, Buffalo's Most Powerful Radio Station, mid-50s letterhead.

Dorothy Ireland was on the air daily as Kay B. Cooke with interviews and homemaking tips. Wally Wagoner was WKBW's Farm Director.

Carroll Hardy, who would go on to become one of WEBR's legendary jazz deejays, was one of the many men who served as WKBW's Clock Watcher, broadcasting live from the front lawn of the radio station on Main Street near Utica every morning.

Among the others on KB's deejay staff in the mid-50s were Herb Knight, George "Hound Dog" Lorenz, and Larry Brownell.

Remembered as one of Buffalo's most beloved sports broadcasters, Stan Barron was also a disc jockey through most of his time in Buffalo radio, including his turn as WKBW's Clock Watcher. Here he's on KB's lawn with Clint Churchill Jr., WKBW General Manager Al Anscombe, KB Polka Beehive host Stan Jasinski, salesman Jim McGrath and Roger Baker— who, after returning to KB from WBES-TV, dabbled in sports but focused on sales.

Stan Barron calling play-by-play action at Memorial Auditorium on WKBW. Through the years, he called Canisius and Niagara basketball, Buffalo Bisons baseball and Buffalo Bisons hockey. He was also the color man on Buffalo Bills broadcasts alongside Van Miller.

Frank Frederics, who also anchored newscasts on WBUF-TV, reads the news on WKBW as engineer William Routh looks on.

Lee Forster brought the sounds of Western music and folk music to KB, as he had also done on Ch.4's Barn Dance show.

From 1958 to 1988, Al Lafler had his hand on the rudder of the production sound that allowed KB to stand head and shoulders above the rest. His more famous co-workers will tell you, his credo "Good enough isn't good enough," helped give KB such a great sound over the years.

232

Gospel musician and evangelist Elder Charles Beck ran his network of 30 stations from WKBW. Nicknamed The Singing Evangelist, The Encyclopedia of America Gospel Music calls Beck "a seminal figure in the formative years of modern African-American gospel music." His shows aired Sunday nights on KB.

Verne Stevenson played the best in rhythm and blues on Saturday nights on WKBW.

Michael Brocia hosted music and news in Italian on Saturdays on WKBW.

Chief Engineer Leroy Fiedler, left, was at WKBW from the very beginning in 1926, and was still with the station through the 60s. Dan Lesniak, right, with Cassie Lanzalaco, was a KB salesman who founded one of the stations that helped usher in the FM era of Buffalo radio as the owner of WADV-FM.

Al Anscombe was a sports announcer under Roger Baker at KB before serving in the Air Corps in World War II. In 1950, he replaced Baker as KB's general manager.

It was under the direction of Al Anscombe that the mostly staid, conservative, WKBW would up-end radio not just in Buffalo but around the country when, as their ad campaign said, "KB Goes KA-BOOM!" introducing a Top-40 style rock 'n' roll format which debuted 19 months after the 30th anniversary of Doc Churchill's WKBW was celebrated in 1956.

From a full-page ad on Ch.2's first day of broadcasting in 1954, showing the hosts of some of the new station's featured live audience programs:

1. **Breakfast for Two with Helen Neville**, *Monday-Friday at 9am.*
2. **Cookin' Cues with Charlotte McWhorter**, *weekdays, 1pm.*
3. **For M'Lady** *with Mari and Gilbert Bass from The Park Lane, Tue &* *Thur at 2:30pm*
4. *Mary Lawton as* **Mother Goose**, *Saturdays at 11am*
5. **Outdoors Inn** *with Ollie Howard, Tuesdays at 7pm*
6. **Dollar Derby** *with Bill Keaton, Wednesdays at 2:30pm*

WGR-TV, Buffalo's Ch.2

Even with UHF stations coming and going, there were no fewer than four competing interests who had applied to the FCC for the license to operate Ch.2. Several of those interests combined to form a new WGR Corporation, which was awarded the license in 1954.

"A bright new channel of television service and entertainment opens up for Buffalo and Western New York today as WGR-TV takes to the air on Channel 2," reported the Evening News on August 14, 1954, with the sign-on of Buffalo's second UHF station.

"Televiewing," reported The Buffalo Evening News," was now a "staple fare" in most homes along the Niagara Frontier. The cost of television sets had dropped precipitously since Ch.4's 1948 sign-on, and having a second reliable station to watch was enough to make many holdouts into television owners.

Longtime Buffalo radio personality Billy Keaton welcomed viewers to the new station—which unlike the other two stations that had signed on the year before, every single one of the 430,000 TV sets in the Buffalo area could watch Ch.2 without a UHF converter box.

Longtime WGR Radio veteran Billy Keaton emceed the opening broadcast ceremonies on WGR-TV, Ch.2.

From a full-page ad that ran in the Courier-Express and The Evening News on the day Ch.2 signed on. Newsmen Roy Kerns and Pat Fagan as well as sportscasters Roger Baker and Bill Mazer were in the spotlight on nightly news and sports programs, and Ollie Howard brought his outdoors show from radio to TV as well.

238

FOR NEWS AND WEATHER IN BUFFALO:

THE UNBEATABLE COMBINATION: Television's most Popular and Respected News Team

ROY KERNS 6:30 - 6:40 LOCAL AND REGIONAL NEWS • JACK MAHL 6:40 - 6:45 THE WEATHER PICTURE • CHET HUNTLEY / DAVID BRINKLEY 6:45 - 7:00 HUNTLEY - BRINKLEY REPORT

EVERY WEEKDAY 6:30-7:00 PM

WGR-TV CHANNEL 2
A TRANSCONTINENT STATION

Authoritative. Respected. Those were the types of adjectives thrown around when describing Roy Kerns, the anchor of Ch.2's early newscasts for most of the station's first decade on the air. "Mr. Kern's polished presentation… is the enjoyable habit of many thousand Niagara Frontier viewers," said a 1956 ad. Kerns left Buffalo for his native Oklahoma City in 1967.

NBC's Chet Huntley and David Brinkley were a heavily marketed part of WGR-TV's news team, so much so that Brinkley visited Ch.2's Barton Street studios to help dedicate a new set in 1964. Here, he's joined by Chuck Poth.

Pat Fagan was a Ch.2 news anchor, as seen here in the early 60s, but he was also the host of the station's Teen Dance Party. Fagan left Buffalo in the mid-60s for an ABC-TV staff announcer position. He began his career at WBNY in 1948. He also worked at WEBR and made appearances as an actor in Ch.4's dramatic series "The Clue."

Checkers & Can-Can was a kid's show produced by Ch.2, airing mornings at 9:30. The actors behind the clown and the "tin-can man" were Philadelphia TV veterans Ed McDonnell, who had been Philly's "Flying Sorcerer," and Joe Earley who had played "Mr. Rivets" on WPTZ-TV Ch.3.

Fantasy Island General Manager Clyde Farnan played Buckskin Joe on a TV version of the park's Wild West Show. He was joined by Marshall Rick, Annie Oakley, Little Bo Peep, and bad guys like Cactus Pete and Black Bart– played by Fantasy Island's business manager Harvey Benatovich.

Bob Lawrence was one of the original cast of announcers when Ch.2 first signed on—his primary job until he left the station 13 years later was as a weatherman.

From the very beginning, however, he was one of the station's kiddie show hosts, first as Captain Atom during the local breaks on the Colonel Bleep cartoon show, and then as Captain Bob during Popeye cartoons and The Mickey Mouse Club.

When the station first signed on, Ch.2's signal was weak into the Southern Tier—so the station's programming was also broadcast on Ch.6 in Jamestown. The problem was later fixed when Ch.2 moved its transmitter facility from Buffalo to the Town of Wales in southern Erie County.

CAPTAIN BOB AND THE MICKEY MOUSE CLUB

2 WGR-TV **6**
CH. BUFFALO   CH. JAMESTOWN

© WALT DISNEY PRODUCTIONS

4-5 PM   MON.-FRI.

Watch **COMPLETE WEATHER NEWS** with BOB LAWRENCE

MON. thru **FRI. – 6:40 pm** & **11:10 pm**
Plus these weekend reports… SAT., 11:10 pm, SUN., 11:10 pm

on **WGR-TV**

CHANNEL **2** BUFFALO

Aside from entertaining the kids and hosting cartoons, Bob Lawrence was Ch.2's lead weather personality through most of the station's first decade.

From 1954 to 1968, Jack Mahl—with his pleasantly deep voice—was another of Ch.2's weathermen. He would go on to anchor radio newscasts on WYSL, WEBR, and WBUF through the 70s and 80s. His rhyming TV sign-off became famous, as he said, "That's all from Mahl" with a salute.

WGR-TV Atlantic Weatherman John Lascalles.

Helen Neville stands in the background as Polish dancers get ready to perform outside the Ch.2 studios on Barton Street.

"Bill Mazer is as good as there is in his chosen profession of reporting interestingly and enthusiastically, sports of all sorts."

After a hitch in the army at the end of World War II, Mazer came to Buffalo in 1947, working first at WKBW and then WGR. During his 16 years in Buffalo, Mazer is best remembered in Buffalo for his long association with the baseball Bisons at Offermann Stadium, but he also called the action for the hockey Bisons and Canisius College basketball from the Aud, as well as Buffalo Bills football from the Rockpile during the All-America Football Conference days in the late 40s.

Along with Roger Baker, he was one of the WGR-TV's original stable of sportscasters when the station signed on in 1954. In 1955, he also hosted the "Watch the Birdie" program, sponsored by Kaufman's Rye Bread on Ch.2. As "Uncle Bill," he made phone calls to kids, giving way prizes between Woody the Woodpecker cartoons.

Born in Ukraine, Mazer grew up in Brooklyn—and returned home to become a beloved New York City sports broadcasting fixture starting in 1964. He was also seen on network broadcasts for CBS and Fox, and played a role as a reporter in the epic 1980 film 'Raging Bull.'

After leaving WEBR, Bob Wells joined the staff at WGR-TV to emcee a handful of popular shows. While Frank Dill was the orginal host of Pic A Polka, Wells hosted with bandleader Frank Wojnorowski for most of the show's run.

Bob Wells also was the original host of Yankee Doodle Time when the show premiered on WGR-TV in 1961. It was the only television show hosted live five days a week in a Buffalo department store.

Jack Tapson was an editor and photographer, who knew– as it was unfolding– that he was watching something important unfolding in front of him daily.

He started at Ch.4 as a lover of photography and teen technician in the 1940s and moved onto Ch.2 where he started the news film department in the mid-1950s.

For decades, these jobs put him on the front lines of some of the really amazing things that were happening in what was then America's 15th largest city, as well as behind the scenes at Buffalo's big TV stations.

Over the period of several years, he shared his memories and photos with next-generation storytellers Marty Biniasz and Steve Cichon.

While The Buffalo Evening News did a tremendous job capturing the story of the WBEN stations in photos, Jack's behind the scenes candid shots from the first 15 years of WGR-TV offer a look at the station which would have otherwise been lost to history. You're enjoying many of these photos in this book because he cared enough to take pictures... and then cared enough to share them.

The WGR-TV mascots were a pair of mischievous elves named Iris and Earis, according to research done by Marty Biniasz for Forgotten Buffalo's website. He reports they were first drawn by Ch.2 art director Frank Wahl as the station signed on.

Guy King ushers in bad boy Rock 'n' Roll

It was the moment that ushered in Buffalo's rock 'n' roll era; the craziest radio prank to date in Buffalo and Tom Clay-- who was one of many men who used the air name "Guy King" on WWOL Radio-- kicked it off in style... and with a visit from the cops.

July 3, 1955 saw a broadcast event that wouldn't even raise an eyebrow 65 years later, but caused fire trucks to be dispatched and a disc jockey arrested in the heart of Downtown Buffalo.

Leading into the Independence Day holiday, "wearing Bermuda shorts and waving a microphone," wrote Buffalo News radio critic Anthony Violanti years later, Guy King "climbed out the window of WWOL and sat atop a billboard, 75 feet above Shelton Square in downtown Buffalo," yelling to the cars below to blow their horns while he played Bill Haley & The Comets' "Rock Around The Clock" over and over.

Tom Clay was arrested after spending time perched atop the WWOL billboard in Shelton Square. Traffic was snarled for hours in what was then considered "Buffalo's Times Square" because of the lights and action. Today, the area little more than MetroRail tracks in front of the Main Place Mall.

Buffalo Police and Buffalo Fire didn't appreciate the prank, and Clay spent part of the night in the clink, but not before Clay turned the mic on and broadcast a scuffle with police—who had earlier promised he wouldn't be arrested if he climbed down.

Despite having done a similar event a few months earlier to raise money for polio research with the blessing of police, this time Clay was charged with two penal code violations: disorderly conduct and creating a disturbance. He was released into the custody of WWOL owner Leon Wyszatycki, but when Clay left the station in the days following his arrest, he was re-arrested and couldn't post the $500 bond. He spent two more nights in jail.

Tuesday, July 5, 1955

DISC JOCKEY ATOP SIGN CAUSES JAM IN SHELTON SQUARE

The antics of a disc jockey atop a sign about 75 feet above Shelton Square Sunday afternoon caused an ear-shattering traffic jam, brought out a fire aerial-ladder truck and four police cars and landed the WWOL employe in jail.

Thomas Clague, 25, of 91 16th St., who broadcasts as Guy King, was charged with disorderly con-
duct after Commissioner DeCillis determined the station had no permit for the demonstration. Police also served Clague with a warrant dated Jan. 7 which charges Clague ignored a parking tag.

He spent more than six hours in the cellblock in Police Headquarters until Assistant Detective Chief Leo V. Swanekamp ordered him released in the custody of City Judge Michael E. Zimmer. King was served with the traffic warrant while in the cell. Police today said Clague will be arraigned tomorrow in City Court. It was the second time Clague
had jammed traffic in Shelton Square and caused an ear-splitting din with his radioed instructions to motorists to honk their horns. On May 8 police allowed his demonstration to continue after Commissioner DeCillis approved it.

The aerial ladder truck was dispatched from Hook & Ladder 2 when a caller telephoned saying that a man was trapped on the roof. Clague, however, made his own way back to the station's studios. The four police cars were necessary to untangle the traffic jam.

From The Buffalo Evening News

"I didn't intend to disturb the peace, I sincerely believed I was doing something to entertain my listeners," Clay told the judge as he pleaded guilty and was fined $25.

"I am not going to punish you very much but this should serve as a warning to others," said Judge Casimer T. Partyka in handing down the sentence.

It should be noted that 16 years earlier on WGR, an upstart disc jockey named Clinton Buehlman would hang out of the window of the Rand Building, and encourage motorists to drive by and honk.

At the time, the Courier-Express reported lightheartedly on Buehlman's exploits.

"Clinton Buehlman is not bothered by fear of high places; he recently perched on the ledge of the eighteenth floor parapet of the Rand Building while his picture was being taken."

Meanwhile, The Buffalo Evening News summed up Clay's time at WWOL as having "created near riots with car parades, worked his audience into a frenzy by playing the same R & R number for long periods of time and... def(ying) police."

Tom Clay in 1959, as he was fired from a Detroit radio station after admitting to accepting payola. Trouble followed him, as he was also run out of town after asking listeners to send a dollar to join a Beatles Fan Club. 80,000 kids sent a buck—most got nothing back.

Clay is best remembered, however, for his 1971 song "What the World Needs Now Is Love"/"Abraham, Martin and John," featuring a blend of the two songs interspersed with audio actualities featuring John Kennedy, Robert Kennedy, and Martin Luther King, Jr.

Once Clay left the station, immediately there was a new "Guy King" on WWOL. The name was the "house name" for the afternoon drive host on the station, and several men used the name on the air.

WWOL, 1956 ad, featuring Fred Klestine, Vic Bell—who'd later broadcast at WKBW as Jack Kelly, and Frank Ward as Guy King.

Guy King #3, Frank Ward, was the man who replaced Clay. He was also known to climb out on billboards— but by the time he was doing it in 1957, law enforcement didn't seem to mind.

Ward and and his fellow WWOL deejay Fred Klestine would climb on top of the Aero Drive-In movie screen during appearances at the Union Road, Cheektowaga location.

Before he was known as Guy King, Frank Ward was popular on WKBW.

Dick Lawrence brings Top-40 to Buffalo

A young program director with a big mouth, big ideas, and a big appetite for promotion *rock 'n' rolled* his way into Buffalo in 1957, and Dick Lawrence permanently etched his taste for music and in-your-face radio into the taste and expectations of Buffalonians.

Even if they came along kicking and screaming. Buffalo's newspaper radio critics reflected the feelings of most Western New Yorkers past the age of 16, with regards to the new sounds coming out of their radios.

Dick Lawrence

Sturgis Hedrick of the Buffalo Evening News recalled Lawrence on the pages of the paper as "the energetic young man who brought the raucous, jangling—and alas, moderately successful—sound of 'modern radio' to Buffalo."

The original WBNY Top-40 line-up included Lawrence, who appeared on the air as Felix with his pet parrot Fernando.

"A sound of hoopla and noisy disc jockeys went into full swing night and day," said the Courier-Express' Jack Allen. "Most 15-minute newscasts, a tradition at the station, were dropped and Gene Korzelius' sportscasts were reduced. The fast-paced schedule eventually also did away with the Grosvenor Library Classical Music Show…The top-40 format with the rock 'n' roll beat was in to stay."

The theme is pretty clear. It was also echoed by J. Don Schlaerth.

"Station WBNY, described as 'the friendly voice of Buffalo' seems to have given in to the noisy bounce of rock 'n' roll and Elvis Presley to 'keep up with 1957 musical tastes.' Not long ago semi-classical music and standard favorites predominated on WBNY. Then there was no room for an Elvis."

Henry Brach was a newsman and deejay at WBNY and as 'BNY's news director, gave Danny Neaverth his first job in Buffalo radio. He moved over to KB and spent more than 20 years there as the station's gruff uncle and the butt of the jokes of untold numbers of disc jockeys.

If you tuned to WBNY in the late 50s, you were likely to hear the voice of Daffy Dan Neaverth, Fred Klestine and Henry Brach. At WBNY, Neaverth would pull a rooftop like event similar to Guy King's, throwing candy out to passersby. Neaverth, perhaps with his boyish good looks and demeanor, evaded arrest for his stunt.

Daffy Dan Neaverth, WBNY. Neaverth left WBNY for WKBW, inspiring the rath of Dick Lawrence—who made firing Neaverth one of his first acts when he became boss at KB. Neaverth went to work at WGR until returning to 1520 for a 26-year run at the station.

It was fast tempo music, fast tempo talk, fast tempo musical station IDs. It was also the only programming on the station. Rock 'n' roll could be heard elsewhere on the dial, but nowhere else was it the only music a station played.

Love it or hate it, the tiny 250-watt station-- which could barely be heard outside of the city's boundaries-- was the talk of Western New York.

Other radio stations hated more than radio critics and parents of teens combined.

Four months into Dick Lawrence's reign at WBNY, WGR announced that it is no longer in the rock 'n' roll business.

"Radio station WGR, after taking an impartial music survey among local housewives, has decided to go off the 'hot' music path into the relaxing realm of 'good music,'" reported The Courier-Express. "It will let other Buffalo stations divide the rock 'n roll spoils."

The survey named Perry Como as favorite male vocalist followed by Pat Boone and Bing Crosby.

The next day, the paper printed reactions from local radio programmers and called Lawrence's response "violent."

"I've seen this policy tried before," Lawrence said. "It doesn't work and I'll be a pallbearer at their funeral."

WGR went to the extreme, but most other stations had some rock music at some point during the day. The only station that didn't, was WBEN.

"The changing styles in music have never affected the WBEN program policy of providing music, news, drama and public service for all members of the family," a station official told the Courier-Express.

Other radio stations might not have embraced the music, but after six

months, they were beginning to lose revenue. 50,000-watt WKBW Radio was losing to a 250-watt station.

WKBW General Manager Al Anscombe told the Courier-Express that the sound being put out by Dick Lawrence was "slightly wacky" – but the trends were there. KB could die on the vine, or go all in.

And did KB go all in. The station owned by a preacher with call letters standing for "Well-Known Bible Witness" hired away the young programmer and promoter who sent a donkey around downtown Buffalo wearing a sign that said, "Everybody is listening to the new WBNY but me, and you know what I am!"

Lawrence christened KB as Futursonic Radio, rock 'n' roll had a new home on Buffalo's radio dial, and KB would begin a dominance that would last a generation.

Within a year of the change to a Top-40 format on July 4, 1958, WKBW Radio was taking out full-page ads in Buffalo's newspapers touting their status as Buffalo's most listened to radio station.

YOU'VE DONE IT **AGAIN!**

Thank You,

BUFFALO

FOR MAKING IT POSSIBLE

THE EVEN NEWER

wKBw

RADIO 1520

1ST

PULSE AND HOOPER AGREE ... SURVEY-PROVEN BUFFALO'S MOST LISTENED-TO RADIO STATION ✱

✱ C. E. HOOPER RADIO AUDIENCE INDEX JULY-AUG.
MON. through FRI. 7 am to 10 pm ALL DAY AVERAGE
✱ PULSE RADIO AUDIENCE REPORT JULY-AUG.
MON. through SUN. 6 am to 12 mid. ALL DAY AVERAGE

One of the most famous disc jockeys to spin tunes on WBNY only lasted about a month at the station-- but would go on to a legendary career in syndicated radio and voice work.

Before he became the voice of "American Top 40" and Shaggy on "Scooby-Doo," Casey Kasem was "Casey at the Mic" on WBNY in 1960. Shortly before his arrival, he set a record at WJW in Cleveland for what he called "world's longest on-air kiss," after laying an 85-second smooch on starlet Diana Trask.

Much later, Kasem would admit to "screwing around too much" during his short time in Buffalo. He'd land in San Francisco, and was well on his way to forever having his feet in the ground while reaching for the stars.

Early group shot of The Even Newer WKBW Futursonic disc jockeys, including Jim Taylor, Ted Hackett, Tom Shannon, Don Keller, Dick Braun, Gene Nelson, Bob Diamond, and Russ Syracuse.

Dick Biondi at a record hop in 1960, just before leaving KB for Chicago.

Dick Biondi was the first nighttime voice of the rock 'n' roll era on WKBW.

He referred to himself as "a screamer," and often told the story about how he was fired from KB because he was too loud. He also claimed to have been fired from KB because he played an Elvis song that wasn't approved.

What really happened: he told listeners that one of KB's managers was driving down Main Street in an Impala convertible. "If you see him," he said, "Throw a rock!"

Someone did—through the boss' windshield. *Maybe he was too loud.*

IT'S TERRIFIC !

"The last big sale was sensational! But this round-the-clock blast at Burnham's is terrific! They've got carloads of deals and I'll be telling you about them on WKBW! Listen for the price smashers!"

DICK BIONDI
WKBW 1520 on dial!

Dan Neaverth, WKBW

Irv Weinstein joined the WKBW Radio news staff in 1958, ultimately becoming the station's news director. He was responsible for creating a news sound that reflected the music and personalities on the station. He walked across the parking lot to become Ch.7's news anchor in 1964.

When WNIA officially signed on in 1956, the station was promised to be "as revolutionary to radio as color was to television."

More than just Top-40, the record library at the Genesee Street studios boasted more than 10-thousand recordings.

But there was still plenty of room for rock 'n' roll. From early on, 1230am was "a home for top tunes" as J. Don Schlaerth put it in the pages of the Courier-Express, who wrote, "as a new station with lots of peppy music, the ratings began to jiggle."

In 1957, Gordon Brown, owner, WNIA, told The Courier-Express, "We play the top 100 tunes half of the time and the old standards the other half of the time. I think people like the sweet popular music as well as rock 'n' roll. We've had terrific results in the popular music field. We also like to play some soft music to help the housewife work around the house."

WNIA

YOUR ALL-MUSIC STATION

TOMMY THOMAS

BOB BELL

WNIA RADIO

JERRY JACK

MIKE MELODY

1230

"Young Adult" RADIO

WNIA signed-on in 1956, and doubled its power in 1962.

While the power changed, what didn't was the disc jockey's names. For more than two decades, when you turned on the radio in the morning, the deejay identified himself as Tommy Thomas— even though it might have been a different guy with a different voice calling himself Tommy Thomas the day before.

Just like with Guy King at WWOL, station founder Gordon Brown insisted that the disc jockeys at the radio stations he owned use those on-air handles instead of their own.

He felt the stock jock names gave a more consistent sound even as the DJs changed rapidly, it was always Mike Melody and Jerry Jack.

WNIA saw itself as *a more staid* (and cheaper!) version of WKBW. KB wasn't mentioned by name in one 1963 ad, but anyone reading it would have known what was being implied.

"As far as wild banshee, screaming announcers, wild nonsense gimmicks and promos... NEVER on WNIA."

At 1080am, WINE was perhaps the least remembered of the handful of radio stations which tried to break in on the Rhythm music scene in late 1950s Buffalo.

"WXRA has changed their call letters along with their programming," wrote Danny McBride in his column in the Blasdell Herald in 1957. "The new call is WINE, along with crazy sounds like the new WBNY."

The WINE call letters didn't last very long. In 1960, WINE became WYSL at 1080am.

1080am was then sold to WUFO, and the WYSL call letters moved to 1400am, displacing the old WBNY.

Tune In For Pleasure!

1080 on your dial becomes...

WINE

"The station that goes to your head"

Musical Selections That Are a Reflection of Public Taste!

News As It Happens!

You're Never More Than 5 Minutes From Music!

A New Taste In Town

Before WXRA became WINE, Tommy Shannon had his first radio job there.

Hernando was the morning man at WXRA, and stayed on at WINE. The mic flag in this photo was edited from saying WXRA to WINE.

Hernando went on to do the all-night show on WGR, after the station "gave up" on giving up rock 'n' roll.

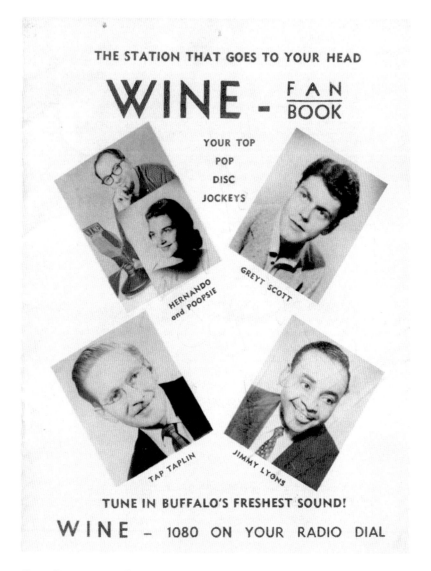

THE STATION THAT GOES TO YOUR HEAD

WINE - FAN BOOK

YOUR TOP POP DISC JOCKEYS

HERNANDO and POOPSIE

GREYT SCOTT

TAP TAPLIN

JIMMY LYONS

TUNE IN BUFFALO'S FRESHEST SOUND!

WINE — 1080 ON YOUR RADIO DIAL

Greyt Scott appeared on other Buffalo stations as Charlie Griggs. Tap Taplin had been a regular on WEBR for at least a decade before moving to WINE, and Jimmy Lyons was Buffalo's first full-time, regularly featured African-American deejay.

The WINE mobile unit—a Volkswagen van—always turning heads.

Disc jockeys joined forces to raise money for charity at a game at the Bishop Timon gym in 1959. Standing: Charlie Griggs (Greyt Scott) WINE, Rog Christian WBNY, Tom Shannon WKBW, Terry Mann WWOL, Dan Neaverth WGR, Danny McBride WEBR, Jack Kelly WKBW, Rick Bennett WWOL. Sitting: Bud Stiker (Jerry Jack) WNIA, Dick Carr WBNY, and Don Fortune WBNY.

267

Western Connections

For 20 years, Sunday nights in many households across the country meant an episode of "Gunsmoke" before the late local news. For 19 of those years, a woman who attended Hamburg Junior High and Amherst Central was one of the stars of the show.

Long before Amanda Blake played Miss Kitty, the saloon-owning love interest of Marshall Matt Dillon from 1955-74, she grew up in Western New York.

Born at Millard Fillmore Hospital on Delaware Avenue, the young "Miss Kitty" began her elementary schooling at Kenmore's Lindbergh Elementary, also living in Hamburg and Amherst until 1946, when her father's job at Curtiss-Wright took the family to California.

A 1960 promotional trip was the actress's first trip back to Western New York since moving out west—but it wasn't her last. She stayed in regular contact with old friends and relatives, and visited several times—including to attend her 40th high school reunion-- before her death in 1989.

Amanda Blake surrounded by her Gunsmoke co-stars, including a young Burt Reynolds, who played Deputy Quint Asper on the show for three seasons. Blake was on Gunsmoke for all but the final season of the show's 20-year run.

Gene Barry starred as Bat Masterson for three years on NBC and Ch.2. On a promotional visit to Buffalo, he was interviewed by Helen Neville on WGR-TV and Dan Neaverth on WGR Radio.

Jack Sharpe and WEBR's Trafficopter

After attending Nichols and serving in World War II, Jack Sharpe returned home to start a career in journalism as a Buffalo Evening News copyboy in 1948.

Jack Sharpe behind the wheel of WEBR's mobile transmitter

He joined WEBR Radio in 1952. Seven years later, he combined his love for on-the-scene reporting with Buffalo's place at the center of the aviation industry by initiating Buffalo's first airborne traffic reports in the WEBR Traffic Copter. He became Buffalo's "flamboyant, outspoken eye in the sky."

Jack Sharpe (right) with Jack Prior of Prior Aviation. Buffalo was the second city in the country to carry airborne traffic reports on the radio.

Sharpe (right) with WNY Safety Conference President Gordon Trank, kicking off Buffalo Safety Week 1962.

Sharpe would scold motorists and highway planners while reporting breakdowns and delays. After one big snowstorm, he saw that instead of attacking the road conditions-- a half-a-dozen city plows were parked outside a restaurant.

"If you're wondering why your streets aren't plowed," he said in a live traffic report, "it's because all the plows are parked at Your Host!"

He kept the helicopter hovering so he could watch the drivers scurry away from their grilled bow ties and back out onto the road.

Sharpe spent 14 years flying over Buffalo's highways until he ran for office in 1973. He'd spent five terms as Supervisor of the Town of Amherst, overseeing that community's continued transformation from a farming community to a suburban population center.

Buffalo's third and final VHF station: WKBW-TV, Ch.7

The fight over who would get the license to operate Buffalo's final VHF station was a protracted one, with several years of hostile exchanges between Dr. Clinton Churchill's WKBW group, a group including the Courier-Express, and the owners of WWOL Radio.

Rev. Clinton Churchill's start in broadcasting came in 1924 when he brought his church choir to perform on WGR Radio in 1924. "A bushel basket" full of mail came in, filled with letters asking for more religious programming— and the checks and cash needed to help make that happen. Churchill is shown here with Buffalo Mayor Frank Sedita.

Once the WKBW-TV group was granted the license, the four months it took them to begin broadcasting was the fastest a US TV station had ever gone from approval to programming.

Hollywood's GREATEST MOVIES . . . Consistently on . . . WKBW TV 7

On November 30, 1958, Buffalo once again became a three-station market after Ch. 59 and Ch.17 both stopped broadcasting, and Ch. 7 joined Ch.2 and Ch.4.

KB bunny

The brief sign-on ceremony was hosted by Rick Azar, who introduced Dr. Churchill and several area religious leaders, before introducing the film "Yankee Doodle Dandy."

Ch.2 had the elves and Ch.7 had "KB Bunny."

An ABC affiliate from the moment the station signed on, Ch.7 went on the air with "a compact staff of three announcers." Stan Barron moved over from WKBW Radio. Both Roger Lund and Rick Azar had been at WBUF-TV, which went dark only weeks before Ch.7 began broadcasting.

The sign-on of Ch.7 ushered in another new era in Buffalo TV. All three stations were now available on every television without the need for special equipment-- and each of the broadcast networks now had a local station to air its programming.

"Competition Keen," read the sub-headline in a piece by J. Don Schlaerth. "Now that three VHF television stations can be received in Buffalo, the keenest programming and advertising competition that has ever existed in this market will begin. It should mean better network and local services for area viewers."

On November 30, 1958 Rick Azar was the announcer who signed on WKBW-TV. Six years later, he'd be joined by Irv Weinstein and Tom Jolls two years after that-- to form the troika that would dominate Buffalo television until the turn of the century.

3 BIG REASONS WHY YOU'LL LIKE NEWS WEATHER and SPORTS on **7**

ROGER LUND
Crisp, accurate reporting of the area's NEWS first, 7:15-7:25 p.m. MON.-FRI. 10:45-10:50 p.m. MON.-FRI.

RICK AZAR
Graphic presentations of national, Western New York and Southern Ontario WEATHER. 7:25 p.m. MON.-FRI. 10:50 p.m. MON.-FRI.

STAN BARRON
SPORTFOLIO 10:55 p.m. MON.-FRI. Stan knows SPORTS inside and out . . . and sports fans enjoy his alert, up-to-the-minute sports reporting.

WKBW-TV

WKBW's first newscaster, Roger Lund started in radio in 1935 as an actor at WGR, was chief announcer at WXRA from 1949-54, and after a year in TV in Elmira, joined WBUF-TV as a news anchor and weather man for two years until the station went dark. He served in the Marine Corps in World War II and Korea.

Stan Barron, WKBW-TV Sports Director, 1958

Stan Barron might best be remembered for his nightly "Free Form Sports" shows on WBEN, but that was the final act in a long career in sports and broadcasting in Buffalo. He came to Buffalo in 1952 and spent nine years at WKBW Radio and TV, working as 1520's morning "Clock Watcher," and Ch.7's first sports director.

Through the years, he called the action for the Bills, the Griffs, and the hockey Bisons, but baseball was always his favorite. In 1956, he was instrumental in helping to bring community ownership to the Buffalo Bisons. Then in 1979, he was one of the leading voices to help bring professional baseball back to Buffalo after a ten-year absence.

Stan joined WBEN in 1967 and was a part of the Bills play-by-play team with Van Miller, Chuck Healy, and Dick Rifenburg. Barron was the "every man" of the group— not an accomplished athlete like Healy or Rife, not a polished, impeccably dressed announcer like Van. His gritty voice and common-sense opinions— always willing to tell you when he thought a team "looked like a bunch of donkeys"— felt like it could have just as easily come from the next bar stool than from the radio.

Stan Barron with Buffalo's National Champion Cyclist Edith Ann Johnson.

Decades after the station first signed on, Bob Costello, Marty Stetter, Bill Hiller, Rick Azar, Norm Schultz, Jack Cook and Steve Zappia were all original employees still working at the station.

Shortly after first signing on, WKBW-TV's "News Central" anchor team was Dave Thomas, weather; Bill Gregory, news; and Rick Azar, sports.

Irv Weinstein reports from South Buffalo's Republic Steel.

Though his primary duties were as WKBW Radio News Director, Ch.7 viewers would catch occasional glimpses of Irv Weinstein's reporting on Ch.7 before he moved over to TV full-time in 1964.

Ch. 7's Don Keller interviews Buffalo Schools Superintendent Dr. Joseph Manch. He signed on WNIA as the first Tommy Thomas in 1956, moving to KB as Dick Biondi's newsman. As Don Keller, the Farm Feller, he delivered agricultural news on WKBW Radio and Ch.7. After being sent to his first fire with a wind-up camera and being told by News Director Hal Youngblood to "point it at the flames," his role evolved into Buffalo's first modern street reporter-- gathering and presenting news and interviews. Later known by his real name Don Yearke, he went on to serve as Ch.4's Chief Photographer through the 80s and 90s.

Bow-tied Paul Thompson, like Yearke, was an early Ch.7 cameraman, who was often seen on-camera conducting interviews.

The Relegated Role of Women, con't.

Almost forty years into broadcasting in Buffalo, not much had changed in where one might expect to hear a woman's voice. Speaking to women about women's issues was about the extent of women's roles. There were growing numbers of exceptions, but they were clearly exceptions.

World War II changed things briefly, but not a lot.

As many of WBEN's announcers went to war, the station took the unprecedented step of (temporarily) hiring a woman as an announcer.

Vera Holly, shortly after leaving WBEN signing on ABC, 1947.

But a 1943 memo from the station's top brass told all emcees, telephone receptionists, and the publicity staff that she was not to be referred to while announcing, that she wouldn't use her name while announcing, and that program hosts should refrain from mentioning her name or identity on the air.

Vera Holly was a very popular entertainer on the station for a decade. She was a singer and emcee on WBEN in the 1930s and 1940s, and had top billing on "International House Party," but wasn't allowed to identify herself for the nearly six months she was reading station breaks and newscasts on WBEN.

A CBS gig on "The Jerry Lester Show" landed her in front of the same microphone as the biggest star of 1943– Frank Sinatra.

"I had a great kick working on the same show as Frank," Holly told The Buffalo Evening News. "Confidentially, he really is cute. And much nicer than I expected."

When she was picked up for a network show in 1946, she was called "one of the most promising young stars of radio." Holly went on to announce her own network programs on Mutual, CBS, and ABC.

A decade later, the advent of TV doubled the number of announcing jobs, but not for women— except for a very particular announcing job at the weather map.

As a genre, the "Weather Girl" made its debut on WBUF-TV in 1956 "in what is billed as an amusing and novel presentation of the temperature readings and weather conditions."

The Courier-Express reported that "an attractive young brunette" would be joining Roger Lund at the weather map on WBUF-TV.

"Beauty and the barometer will meet Monday evening on Ch. 17 when Joy Wilson of Kenmore becomes Buffalo's first TV weather girl on a new five-minute program telecast weekdays at 6:45." Wilson worked in the station's office.

Joy Wilson, WBUF-TV "Weather Girl," 1956

Around the same time, Janice Okun was the Milk for Health spokeswoman during WBUF-TV's newscasts, bringing television experience from her time as the second host of Ch.4's "Plain and Fancy Cooking."

She later appeared for the Dairy Council on Ch.7's "Farm & Home" before moving to The Buffalo Evening News as Food Editor.

Janice Okun

It was another woman, however, who combined being the Milk for Health "milkmaid" along with delivering the weather forecast.

Without the benefit of doppler radars or advanced computer imagery, Paula Drew would read the same information provided by the Weather Bureau like any other (male) announcer, and follow the forecast with a live commercial for Western New York's dairy farmers.

At various times through the 1950s, her reports as "The Milk for Heath Milkmaid" were seen on Chs. 2 and 4.

In 1959, dressed in a fur stole and a pill box hat, Drew was received at the White House, bearing a gift for President Eisenhower from the Niagara Frontier's milk producers. The 8-day-old Holstein came from the Genesee County dairy farm of Clarence Johncox.

The elegant Paula Drew also made regular appearances at the Fort Erie Race Track through the 1950s, always wearing pearls and mink, even in the barns.

Drew was also part of a New York State dairy contingent that toured European dairy farming and production facilities. In reporting back to Chautauqua County's dairymen, she told the group that she "drinks at least three glasses of milk per day ... although she likes coffee, tea and an occasional highball when on a date."

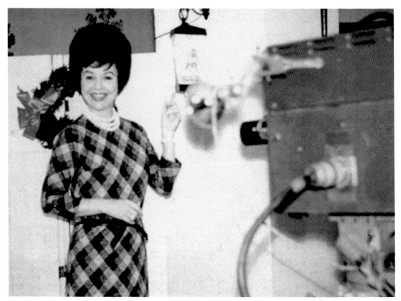

Paula Drew on an AM&A's remote, Ch.2

An accomplished opera singer, Drew attended Juilliard School of Music, training as a coloratura soprano. While attending Juilliard, she was signed to a Universal Pictures contract.

In post-war 1940s Hollywood, she made movies with Red Skelton and Hugh Beaumont — better known later for his role as Ward Cleaver. After working in Buffalo for most of the 1950s, Drew moved onto other corporate public relations work in Toronto. Her last regular gig in Buffalo was as the voice of Tops Friendly Markets through the 1970s until 1983.

Doris Jones modelling Buffalo's own Birge Wallpaper.

Though she broke into TV as model and women's host, Doris Jones was eventually Buffalo's first woman staff announcer.

For Fashion and Household Hints- plus Good Music

LISTEN TO
DORIS JONES
"WHLD's Latest Disc Jockey"

• • • •

Well Known Fashion Model and TV Demonstrator— with Songs and Styles

• • • •

Monday Through Friday 12:30 to 1:00 P. M.

WHLD 1270 on the dial

Jones was still in high school when she started modelling on Ch.4 and later was short-lived WBES-TV's "All Weather Gal" sponsored by Phoenix Beer.

Doris Jones hosted a radio show on WHLD starting in 1957.

As Ch.7 signed on the air, she was "femcee" of the station's daily audience participation show *For the Ladies*, "a pleasant half-hour planned for the housewife," reported the Courier-Express as the show debuted in 1959. "It includes interesting fashion news, a fair sample of live music and assorted singing and dancing. Blonde Doris Jones is the charming hostess."

In 1965, she was hired as a "weathergal" at Ch.2, but union rules dictated she become a full-time staff announcer— making her Buffalo's first woman in that role. She wound up doing weather during the 6pm news, anchoring local newscasts during the Today Show, emceeing a Fantasy Island kids show, giving skiing and boating reports, and hosting "TV's first card game," Pay Cards.

Public Broadcasting comes to Buffalo

When the National Broadcasting Company gave up on its Buffalo UHF experiment and pulled the plug on WBUF-TV Ch.17, they sold off all the station's assets but one—the license.

NBC donated the license to broadcast on Ch.17 to the Western New York Educational Television Association, which signed on WNED-TV on March 30, 1959 as New York State's only public television station.

WNED-TV —which stands for Western New York Educational TV— began broadcasting with, what one station official described as "mismatched hand-me-down equipment held together by hope, dumb luck, and quite literally, masking tape... The 'technical difficulties' slide should have read 'financial difficulties.'"

The station's camera blew-out 30 seconds into the first broadcast.

A young John Zach operates a WNED-TV camera. Zach would go on to a career in radio news at WKBW, WGR, and WBEN that would span more than five decades.

Still, "The cultural appeal of the station was immediate," reported Sturgis Hedrick in The News, as Buffalo's Martha Graham Dancers were the first performers featured on the station.

It was touch and go for the first few years, with threats of programming cuts and layoffs of the already barebones staff, but over the station's first decade on the air, WNED-TV saw "increased public support, state support and the greater recognition of public television's role by the federal government."

Starting in the old cinderblock building behind what is the Ch.4 studio today-- WNED-TV moved to the penthouse of the Lafayette Hotel by the end of 1959.

Six local colleges joined with the station to create programming that would allow students to gain college credit through lessons learned on what could hardly be called "the boob tube" when tuned to Ch.17.

Board Chairman Laurence Goodyear reflected, "The services which Ch. 17 has provided to the community have been unique and distinctive."

Bertha Hoffman teaches a French class on Ch.17.

Sister Jeanne, art professor at Rosary Hill College, teaches a class over WNED-TV.

Aside from grammar school, high school, and college credit programs, there were also typing classes, along with training for fire and police. Jack Call was the instructor on Ch.17's "Train for Fire."

Diane Sina was the host of "Type Right" on Ch.17.

*For all the educational programming on WNED-TV, among the favorite
and most watched programs was "Piano on a Terrace," when announcer
Matt Regan would play in the open air on the roof of the Lafayette Hotel.*

*Jack Paupst's
jolly shopkeeper
Mr. Whatnot was
the most popular
show in the
station's early
days.*

Among WNED-TV's original employees was publicity manager J. Michael Collins. He'd become the station's manager, and in 50 years of creating a public broadcasting empire, he'd also become a familiar face during pledge breaks and events like "the Great TV Auction." He's shown here with other staffers who survived the station's first decade: Chief Engineer Gordon Knaier and Technical Operations Director G. Robert Bakaysa.

J. Michael Collins with two young WNED fundraisers.

WBFO-FM signed on in January, 1959, as a student-run, non-commercial, educational radio station at UB. "Classical music, poetry, symposiums and area college news" were on the schedule as the station only broadcast during the evening hours when first on the air.

Electrical engineering students built the studio in the Baird Music Building and a transmitting plant atop the Tower Dormitory.

"The student body benefits internally with the acquisition of broadcasting knowledge by the WBFO staff," said Jack Mettauer, WBFO's first program director, who was also a math student and a former WEBR engineer. "Externally, the wide variety of programs will stimulate student interest in specific fields."

Programming in October, 1959 included an hour of "pop tunes" each night—but *"not to include Top-40 music,"* followed by an hour of news from around the campus and around the world.

WBFO Chief Engineer Howie Barker at the controls, 1959

As the 60s wore on, WBFO found itself in the midst of the unrest on the UB campus, and became a pioneer in public radio as it's known today.

Ch.7's Main Street studios on a snowy night in the late 50s.

WBNY's bright red "News from Where It Happens" cruiser, with "Flash Mike and the Mike Patrol."

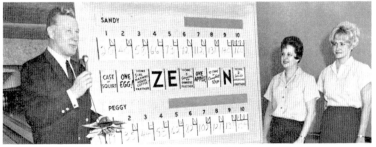

Chuck Healy goes over prizes like a case of Squirt and TV dinners on Strikes, Spares, and Misses on Ch.4.

Henry Brach (with dark glasses) broadcasting live from Sattler's with WBNY deejay Mark Edwards.

Engineers Harold Smith and Leroy Fiedler in the WKBW master control room in the mid-1950s.

WBUF-TV weather personalities Joy Wilson and Mac McGarrity share a laugh.

The Kenneth Baumler family won a 1959 Studebaker Lark in WBNY's "Lark Hunt" contest, sponsored by Buffalo's six-area Studebaker dealers.

Bill Mazer called Bisons games on WKBW before moving to WGR. This team photo, with Mazer superimposed in the top right corner, was taken at Offermann Field in the early 50s. The Bisons moved to War Memorial Stadium in 1960.

WBEN's staff announcers in the late 50s included, standing, Jack Ogilvie, Lou Douglas, Van Miller, Ken Philips, Gene Kelly, Virgil Booth, Clark Erickson, and Bernie Sadler. Harry Webb and Mike Mearian are among those seated.

WKBW's team of disc jockeys, about 1960.

Bob Diamond was a utility man on WKBW, at various times holding down the overnight shift, weekends, the farm report, and production work from the late-50s through the mid-60s.

As a member of the boys' choir singing on WGR starting in 1926, Ed Tucholka's first announcing job was on the PA at Sattler's, 998 Broadway—talking about the bargains of the day, paging mothers of lost children and generally keeping things moving without benefit of a script.

Soon, his deep rich voice would be heard on WEBR, and in over 20 years there, he hosted the wartime "Noon Day Review" highlighting local GIs and as well as Uncle Ed's Children's Hour.

After stops at WWOL and WHLD, Tucholka moved to the WBEN stations in 1966 and oversaw WBEN-FM, always reflecting simple dignity and elegance he presented on the radio for nearly 70 years.

WBEN Operator/Engineer Tom Whalen gets ready to cue up albums for Clint Buehlman.

News anchor John Corbett looks over news scripts hot off the typewriter of Fran Lucca in the Ch.4 newsroom.

WBEN's Sports team: Dick Rifenburg, Chuck Healy, Van Miller, and Ralph Hubbell. When injury ended Rifenburg's professional football career with the Detroit Lions, the former All-American Michigan wide receiver turned to broadcasting and spent nearly 30 years at WBEN Radio and TV.

Officially, they were Memorial Auditorium and War Memorial Stadium, but to Buffalonians they were *the Aud* and *the Rockpile,* and they were the great WPA-built stone homes of Buffalo's greatest diversions: football, hockey, boxing, basketball, and wrestling.

The men in this photo and their compatriots across the radio and TV dials helped bring those diversions closer. Maybe more than in other cities, Buffalo's sports guys have always been among the most popular broadcasters, as they seemed like one of us while helping to bring us closer to heroes on the court, on the field, in the ring, and on the ice through their work.

With the smooth melodious voice of a classic announcer, Ward Fenton joined WBEN as a radio news man in 1941. After serving in World War II, he returned to the station and was named chief announcer in 1947. He was also heard as the announcer on the NBC network program Mr. IQ, which originated from Shea's Buffalo Theater for a national audience.

His fluency in French, German, and Italian made him a natural for decades' worth of announcing classical music programs, especially on WBEN-FM.

When Ch.4 signed on, he was the station's weekend weatherman, and by the 1960s, was regularly seen in front of the weather map in living rooms all over Western New York, with his forecasts sponsored by the Charles R. Turner Company. His segments were bookended with a memorable film clip showing trucks at the Turner's company garages. At the beginning of the weather segment, the trucks headed out onto the street, and then after the weather forecast, the same film ran in reverse, with the trucks appearing to back into the garage.

Fenton became Ch.4's Chief Announcer in 1967, and retired in 1975.

Harry Webb anchors a WBEN-TV newscast sponsored by Esso, and interviews Massachusetts Senator John F. Kennedy on a visit to Buffalo in 1958.

Buffalo's visits to Romper Room

★

STARTS MONDAY

★

A **New** TV Program For Pre-School Youngsters

Meet MISS PAT, a highly qualified teacher with wide experience with children . . . including being the mother of three of her own.

"ROMPER ROOM"

with **MISS PAT**

The "ROMPER ROOM" School is a program that parents and educators in **46** cities agree is an invaluable aid to the development of your child's personality.

ACTIVITIES ON "ROMPER ROOM" INCLUDE:

● Prayer Time
● The Pledge of Allegiance to the Flag
● The Rhythm Band
● Story Time
● Look 'n' See
● Teach-It Project
● Show 'n' Tell
● Singing Games
● Let's Gallop—a new educational feature
● The Famous & Fabulous "Mr. Do Bee"

MON. - FRI. 9:30 A.M.

WGR-TV   CHANNEL 2

★

In 1956, Miss Pat was the first Buffalonian to end Romper Room with... "I see Patrick... and Marie... and Jane... and Phillip..."

Through the 50s, 60s, and 70s, there were around a dozen different versions of the Romper Room franchise seen in Buffalo living rooms.

There were nationally syndicated versions aired on Buffalo stations, as well as local shows that were produced in Toronto and Hamilton easily seen in Western New York with rabbit ears and maybe a bit of tin foil.

But on three different occasions—on three different stations-- there were Buffalo-produced Romper Room shows with Mr. Do Bee and the "magic mirror" as well.

Ch.2 aired its version of Romper Room starting in 1956 with Miss Pat as host. Par Schrier was a teacher in the North Tonawanda schools.

After a two-year run, Ch.7 picked up the show with a new host, Miss Mary. Her real name was Cele Klein, and she'd been a veteran soap opera actress. The show would get 150 letters a day from kids across WNY and Southern Ontario.

Miss Mary, Cele Klein, left, and Miss Binnie Liebermann, right.

She handed her magic mirror over to Miss Sally Klein, who was around for about a year, then Miss Binnie Liebermann, who was hosting the show when the local version was cancelled in 1962– "clobbered" in the ratings, according to Channel 7, by Uncle Mike Mearian on Channel 4.

Doris Jones frequently filled in for Miss Binnie towards the end of the show's run.

Another local version of Romper Room came in 1971 when Channel 29 first signed on the air. Miss Elaine Murphy was the host.

Boost Buffalo... It's good for you!

Starting in 1960, Buffalo radio and television stations were donating an estimated $30,000 per month in commercial airtime for the Chamber of Commerce's "Boost Buffalo" campaign.

What's the best home town of all? Winter, Summer, spring and fall?

Buffalo! Buffalo! Boost Buffalo it's good for you!

Boost Buffalo it's good for you! Buffalo's ideal for work or play! Buffalo's ideal in every way!

There's plenty to boast about in Buffalo!—The Boost Buffalo Jingle

"Boost Buffalo" was everywhere.

Commercials blared on radios and TVs, and also filled were billboards and the back of cars-- with 10,000 bumper stickers printed, all organized by the marketing men of Buffalo.

"Some people poke fun at the 'Boost Buffalo, it's good for you' slogan," a chamber official said, "but that only shows that it's caught on, that everybody's heard of it, and that it's good."

Among the Election Day 1960 races being covered closely by Carl Erickson on Ch.4 were between Richard Nixon and John Kennedy for President as well as Edward Rath and Chester Gorski for Erie County Executive.

Erickson came to WBEN in 1948, and was the newsman on Clint Buehlman's show.

He spent most of the 50s and 60s as Chief Announcer for WBEN Radio.

WBEN AM-FM-TV's new home, 1960

A new era in broadcasting was ushered in 1960 when WBEN opened its new studios on Elmwood Avenue. WBEN AM-FM-TV had outgrown the studios it had called home on the 18th floor of the Statler Hotel since 1930.

The Buffalo Evening News stations bought the former WBUF-TV studios, which had been built by NBC only a few years earlier, and added more studio space and an office building to the complex.

Bill & Mildred Miller show off the stove in their new studio, 1960

Clint Buehlman, operator Tom Whalen, and engineer Earnest Roy— who started with the station before it even went on the air in 1930– are shown in the new, far more spacious radio studios.

WBEN announcers Carl Erickson and Jack Ogilvie are seated as Mike Mearian leans on the piano of Norm Wullen, 1960.

WBEN executives George Torge, Alfred Kirchhofer, station owner Kate Butler, James Righter, and C. Robert Thompson inspect the new WBEN-TV control room. The $1.5 million building was heralded as the "most modern broadcasting center in the nation." The final broadcast from the Statler was Jan. 10, 1960.

After WNED-TV left for the Lafayette Hotel, the studios for WGR Radio were in the building behind WBEN's studios in the late 50s and early 60s.

It's incredible to think that when Van Miller started calling the play-by-play for the brand-new Buffalo Bills of the American Football League in 1960, he was better known as Ch.4's 11pm news and weather announcer than a sports broadcaster. Through two AFL straight championships, four straight Super Bowls, and two stadiums, Van's sense of the game and amplified level of excitement became the filter through which football-loving Buffalo took their love to the next level. He'd call every game during the NBA Buffalo Braves' stay in the city and work as Ch.4's primary sportscaster for more than 30 years. "Do you believe it?" he'd ask, as fandemonium went into overdrive, imploring "fasten your seatbelts!" until retiring as the Voice of the Bills after 37 years in 2003.

A new voice for Buffalo's Black community: WUFO

"Buffalo's newest radio voice spoke in its debut with a sound of moderation and sincerity, and promised an ambitious public service program," reported Jack Allen in the Courier-Express as WUFO signed on at 1080am.

Eddie O'Jay   Jimmy Lyons   George Lorenz   Joe Rico

WUFO's original on-air staff, 1961

Since 1961, WUFO's programming has remained 100% dedicated to Buffalo's Black community, which had grown 143% from 1950-1960.

"The only Black-owned and operated radio station in Buffalo and the only source of music and information reflective of the black experience," said a 1981 station promotional piece.

Jimmy Lyons with Sammy Davis Jr.

In signing on, WUFO brought to the airwaves Buffalo's first two full-time African-American disc jockeys.

The Courier-Express called Jimmy Lyons "the Jackie Robinson of Buffalo Broadcasting."

When this photo of Jimmy Lyons was taken in the WXRA studios on Niagara Falls Boulevard in Amherst, he was Buffalo's first (and only) black disc jockey.

By the time WUFO signed on, Lyons was a Buffalo radio and entertainment veteran who was first heard on local radio in 1937, when he won the Shea's Buffalo Amateur show on WBEN in 1937 at the age of 17.

Through the '40s, Lyons was a singer and dancer at nightclubs in Buffalo and across the northeast with a stint as an Army lieutenant in between, serving in Italy and Germany during World War II.

After settling back in Buffalo, Lyons became a draftsman for Bell Aircraft, while also entertaining in nightclubs and picking up weekend radio work at small stations around Buffalo like WWOL, WXRA and WINE where he was a pioneer in playing a mix of rhythm and blues and gospel music.

On WUFO, he hosted "The Upper Room" with gospel music twice a day and "The Lyons Den," with R&B music middays.

Bob Wells wasn't the only deejay to host dances at the Dellwood Ballroom.
Jimmy Lyons with Sam Cooke and fans at the Dellwood, Main at Utica.

Ellicott District Councilman King W. Peterson, WXRA owner Ted
Podbielniak, Jimmy Lyons, and attorney (and future councilman and
judge) Wilbur Trammell celebrate Lyons' work in the African-American
community.

Eddie O'Jay came to Buffalo from Cleveland as WUFO's program director and daily "Blues for Breakfast" host.

Eddie O'Jay (left).

He would later hold the same on-air job at New York City stations WWRL and WLIB. His fast-paced pioneering style in Buffalo and then New York inspired many aspiring young African-Americans, including Frankie Crocker and Imhotep Gary Byrd.

Both Crocker and Byrd were Buffalo natives who listened to O'Jay on WUFO, got disc jockey jobs at WUFO themselves, and then followed O'Jay to fame at WLIB in New York City.

When O'Jay died in 1998, both Crocker and Byrd attended his funeral and spoke to the New York Daily News.

"When I was growing up in Buffalo," said Byrd, "there were no black radio stations and no black jocks. Eddie O'Jay was the first black voice I heard on the radio. He hit that town like a tornado."

Crocker said of his mentor, "The deejay was the show. You never looked at the clock. When the record ended, you talked, and Eddie was a master. He's the reason I went into radio."

Gary Byrd, 1975

The most widely remembered claim to fame for O'Jay, whose real name was Edward O. Jackson, was the soul group the O'Jays.

The group that scored several hits in the '70s including "Love Train" was formed in the '50s as the Mascots. They renamed themselves the O'Jays in honor of the disc jockey after he began to heavily promote their music on the radio in the early 1960s.

O'Jay and Lyons starred in a series of radio commercials for Simon Pure Beer, where Lyons was aboard a spaceship called the "East Aurora," which was fueled by Simon Pure Beer.

When WUFO first signed on, Courier-Express critic Jack Allen wrote, "O'Jay has arranged, along with Lyons, a schedule of daily broadcasts

which at first listening seem conservative and in excellent taste, and which should gain wide appeal with its constructive service contributions to the community."

Luckily for the nearly six decades of great radio it inspired, WUFO from its very earliest days has remained excellent in taste, but has veered from the conservative to the innovative more often than not.

WUFO newsman Malcom Erni

O'Jay spent about a year at WUFO and was replaced by Sunny Jim Kelsey. Soon after, Frank Crocker became a regular in WUFO's lineup.

Sunny Jim Kelsey, WUFO

Frankie Crocker... Chief Rocker... The Eighth Wonder of the World!!! Revered as the man who changed the rules for African-Americans as both disc jockeys and musicians, Frankie Crocker started down the road to national fame via New York City and nationwide reverence from his native Buffalo.

A graduate of Buffalo's East High School, Crocker was studying pre-law at UB when he was bitten by the radio bug, joining WUFO as News Director in 1964. There, he tasted early success spinning urban wax and never turned back.

Francis Crocker, East High Class of 1958

As a deejay at New York City stations WWRL, WMCA and WBLS, Crocker began playing album cuts and extended mixes from Urban artists, bringing a more diverse sound to the airwaves and opening the door for more creativity and wider audiences for artists of color. Adding to his cache, was the time he entered New York's famous Studio 54 on white stallion.

Starting with his time in his native Buffalo at WUFO, Crocker helped to bust stereotypes and bring the music of an entire race from the remote corners of the music world to the popular choice of hip New Yorkers.

Frankie Crocker, at New York's WWRL Radio shortly after leaving WUFO Radio in the mid-60s.

After Gordon McLendon bought WBNY 1400am and moved his WYSL call letters over to the station in 1961, WUFO Radio took over WYSL's old spot at 1080am. The call letters at that frequency changed from WXRA to WINE to WYSL to WUFO in a matter of four years, but have remained WUFO for six decades.

WINE's format was Top 40 rock 'n' roll, but WYSL was "beautiful music" when the station first signed on. By the end of the 1960s, WYSL was WKBW's primary Top 40 rock 'n' roll competitor.

When the Boulevard Mall opened in 1962, it was the first to offer "weatherproof shopping" in an enclosed mall space in Western New York.

WEBR deejays Jack Eno, Carrol Hardy, Al Meltzer and others broadcast live from the mall during its first days open to the public.

The Sound of the City: WEBR

After being the first in the nation to attempt a poorly received "sing-along" format, WEBR rebooted its image in 1962 with the new "The Sound of the City" theme song.

The Courier-Express' Jack Allen called The Sound of the City "a bit of good music a cut above the jarring jingles so often associated with commercial AM radio."

"The Sound of the City" was originally written for San Francisco radio station KSFO, which was owned by Gene Autry, and resung for radio stations around the country.

Johnny Mann-- best known as the music director on the Joey Bishop Show-- wrote the song which was performed by "The Johnny Mann Singers."

Among those nameless faceless Johnny Mann singers was Thurl Ravenscroft, who was the singing voice of "The Grinch" with Boris Karloff's narration. Also, as Tony the Tiger, he bellowed out "They'rrrrre GREAT!" on Frosted Flakes commercials for 30 years.

His deep throaty vibrato is easy to pick out in the line, "faint is the thunder of Niagara, soft is the murmur from the lake."

Lyrics to "The Buffalo Anthem," as sung by *The Johnny Mann Singers*

The Sound of the City,
the Good Neighbor City,
the Sound of Buffalo.

Are mixed with daylight's glimmering rays,
and moonbeams shimmering glow.

When darkness settles on the city,
 night sounds slowly come awake.

Faint is the thunder of Niagara,
soft is the murmur from the lake.

Hear the Sound of the city,
the sounds that are heard in Buffalo, New York.

WEBR, Buffalo

One of America's Two Great Radio Stations: WKBW

Riding a wave started with a change to a personality driven Top-40 format in 1958, KB dominated Buffalo radio for most of the next two decades.

Sold by station founder Doc Churchill to national broadcasting powerhouse Capital Cities, the wealthy corporate backing of KB's monstrous 50,000-watt signal helped lead to the evolution of one of the finest examples of a full-service Top-40 station that ever existed.

Eventually grabbing as much as 50% of the market share, KB quickly blew all of the much smaller Top-40 competitors out of the water. Half of the audience was listening to KB. Never before, and never since, has a radio station been so dominant in Buffalo.

Left to right: Don Keller (Yearke), Tom Shannon, Doug James, Wayne Stitt, Jay Nelson, Russ "The Moose" Syracuse, Dan Neaverth, Tom Saunders

The station's base of homegrown talent sprinkled with some of the most talented people from around the country, helped build an unprecedented following for KB in Buffalo and around the country.

The first of those homegrown talents to leave a legacy was the great Tom Shannon, South Buffalo's breaker of hearts and as smooth a disc jockey as Buffalo, Detroit, Denver, LA, or anywhere else has ever known.

Tom Shannon, in the WKBW air studio

Easy to listen to, debonair and literally the boy next door, the handsome and ultra-cool Shannon was a graduate of Holy Family grammar school and Bishop Ryan High.

As if owning nights on KB and driving a Corvette convertible wasn't enough, there was the night Swedish sex-symbol Ann-Margret was in Buffalo on a promotional tour, and hopped in Tommy's sports car for a date at the trendy Candy Cane Lounge, downtown next door to the Market Arcade.

That was the same nightclub where Shannon met the group that would ultimately become known as "The Rockin' Rebels," who would take "Wild

Weekend," their instrumental version of the Tommy Shannon Show theme song, to the national record charts.

At KB, he started as a weekend jock and fill-in guy, and didn't even rank high enough to get his own theme song. It's part of the KB magic that his self-produced, garage-band sounding musical opening touting "Top tunes, news and weather, so glad we could get together, on the, Tom Shannon Show" could become a nationwide Top Ten hit.

Shannon was at Fort Dix doing a hitch in the Army when he heard his song come on the radio and almost couldn't believe it.

Tom Shannon sits in the WGR studio, holding a copy of the Rockin Rebels' Wild Weekend album.

"It was so exciting to be a part of Buffalo radio back then," Tom Shannon said in 1996. "Sometimes the disc jockeys were more popular than the rock stars."

He was bigger than life hosting the night shift on KB, and Buffalo's teens couldn't get enough of Tommy. In 1961, tickets to his "Buffalo Bandstand" TV show on Ch.7 were being counterfeited and new procedures had to be put in place after the number of kids on the dance floor swelled out of control.

While a deejay at KB, Shannon hosted Buffalo Bandstand on Ch.7. When he later moved to WGR Radio, he hosted Hit or Miss on Ch.2.

Tom Shannon hosts a WKBW Record Hop, with Paul Simon, left.

Your days in the sun ... lots more fun with

50 50

QUEEN-O
Quality

SOL LENZNER CORP.

Take 50/50 along today ... the cool new taste of grapefruit and lime drives thirst away ... makes living gay!

Tom Shannon appeared in a series of 1964 print ads for Queen-O.

After spending the 60s and the 70s moving around the country and around radio dials, Shannon was back in Buffalo for his 30th grammar school reunion at Holy Family on South Park at Tifft when he stopped by his old home, WKBW.

A week of fill-in work lead to a three year stay towards the end of KB's run as one of Buffalo's most dominant radio stations. After spending time as a host on the Shop at Home cable TV network, Tommy made it back for one more turn at the air chair in Buffalo hosting afternoon drive on Oldies 104 during the 1990s and 2000s.

From 1960's "WKBW 6-midnight platter and chatter show" host, to 1997's deejay with "a warm conversational tone and knowledge of music and performers," Tom Shannon has been one of the leading voices of Buffalo's baby boomers through every stage of life.

Joey Reynolds,
WKBW

If there was a way to "one up" having your theme song land on the national charts, the guy who eventually followed Shannon in KB's evening slot probably found it.

Joey Reynolds, KB's night man through the mid-'60s, got The Four Seasons to sing their No. 1 hit "Big Girls Don't Cry" with the lyrics changed to "The Joey Reynolds Show." *What a show!*

Another local guy, Reynolds grew up in Buffalo's Seneca-Babcock neighborhood playing radio announcer at the neighborhood Boys Club, and was every bit of a shock jock 20 years before the term was created for Don Imus and Howard Stern.

Joey Reynolds interviews Bobby Sherman on Ch.7's Joey Reynolds Show.

He started a boisterous on-air feud with The Beatles and refused to play their records or even say their name, calling them "the four norks from England." The feud lasted until there was money in it for him-- he helped promote the local band The Buffalo Beatles.

Reynolds' bombastic and over-the-top style earned him a following complete with membership cards for the "Royal Order of the Night People." That audience extended far beyond Buffalo and Western New York. Despite working at a station 300 miles away in Buffalo, he was one of the most popular radio personalities in Baltimore, with thousands of listeners of KB's strong signal mixed with Reynolds' big mouth.

Reynolds' eventual exit from WKBW is one of the most fabled in the legends of radio.

As the 1966 Variety Club Telethon aired on Ch.7, Reynolds felt slighted for being slotted to host the overnight portion of the big event.

One of many memorable stunts orchestrated by Reynolds involved him grabbing Fred Klestine as a tag-team partner to take on the tough, mean Gallagher Brothers in a wrestling match at the Aud.

In his memoir "Let a Smile Be Your Umbrella ... But Don't Get a Mouthful of Rain," Reynolds admits to having had a few drinks before going on radio and giving TV star Frank Gorshin a hard time in an interview about the fundraiser.

Reynolds then insinuated another TV star and telethon guest host – Forrest Tucker of "F Troop" – was a drunk and had a case of booze in his dressing room.

One of the station managers took the episode personally – especially after Reynolds goaded him and made a joke about his bald head.

Seeing the writing on the wall, Joey put the writing on the door.

Rather than waiting to be fired, Reynolds, in an all-time display of brassiness, nailed his shoes to the station manager's door with a note saying "FILL THESE" attached.

Joey Reynolds, Tommy Shannon and Danny Neaverth all grew up in South Buffalo. Reynolds and Neaverth knew each other from St. Monica's, the Babcock Street Boys Club and Timon High School. When teamed up on KB, the cross-talk between Neaverth's afternoon show and Reynolds' evening wrap was the subject of homeroom and lunch table discussion at every Western New York high school the next day, but was also the talk of water coolers and coffee break tables at businesses as well.

Beyonce. Bono. Cher. Some personalities are so renowned and celebrated just one name will do. Such is Buffalo's Danny.

Danny Neaverth is perhaps Buffalo's greatest pop culture star. He's remembered most for peeking at us through the hole in the record behind the microphones of upstart WBNY radio in the 1950s as Daffy Dan, then WGR Radio, and then 26 years at WKBW Radio — with most of those years as Buffalo's morning man. Tag on a dozen more years at WHTT, and a few more at KB again, and Danny moved our fannies on the radio for half a century.

But it wasn't just radio — Neaverth was also a TV weatherman on Ch.7 and later Ch.2.

He was the public address announcer for the NBA Braves and the NFL Bills.

A few of his moonlighting gigs dovetailed more closely with his work as a disc jockey and radio host.

Danny signs hands at a Thruway Plaza record hop.

He was a concert promoter and recording artist (who could forget "Rats in My Room," even if they tried?).

Of course, his face and voice were everywhere for Bells Supermarkets and dozens of other Western New York businesses through the years. His work in the community for dozens of causes and charities over the last 60 years has been unmatched.

In the '70s and '80s, it was difficult to spend a day in Buffalo and not somehow be graced by the voice, smile and personality of "Clean Dan Neaverth," a true Buffalonian who never forgot his Seneca Street South Buffalo roots and proudly plied his trade among fellow Buffalonians proud to call him one of us.

Danny took over mornings from Stan Roberts.

Stan Roberts at the KB mic.

Stan first woke up Buffalonians at WKBW from 1962-70, and then at WGR from 1972-82. He became "the first major Buffalo morning man to make the move to the FM band" when he joined WBUF-FM in 1982. After seven years at WBUF, Stan took WBUF mornings to the number one spot in the ratings— and the very next day, he jumped back to AM, hosting afternoon drive and working in sales at WBEN.

As WGR's morning man, he narrated "Great Sabre Highlights" on the flip side of the very successful record single, Donna McDaniels' "We're Gonna Win That Cup." Stan also wrote at least two joke books, including "Sabres Knock-Knocks."

Stan still hasn't lived down the early 80s Royalite television commercial where he put a lampshade on his head, and in the late 80s, when, as the

Bills PA announcer, he had to implore fans to "please stay off the field" while they stormed the Rich Stadium field, taking down the goalposts to celebrate the Bills' clinching the AFC East in 1990.

The warm friendly voice of Fred Klestine felt like a cup of cocoa near the fire.

Fred Klestine, right, visits Xavier's Meats at the Broadway Market

"An institution in Western New York," his radio career when he was working at Lackawanna's Bethlehem Steel, and a manager at Lackawanna's WWOL heard his voice and told him to audition. Deejay was considerably easier than working in a blast furnace, and Fred spent the next 40 years keeping Buffalo company.

In the 50s, Klestine worked at WWOL and WBNY, before his long famous run at KB Radio. He was later heard on WADV-FM, and then on WBUF-FM through most of the 80s.

Then there was Pulse Beat News. Irv Weinstein was the news director and spiritual leader of the KB's news staff.

"In terms of style, I was sometimes asked who my idol was in radio, and that was an easy one: Paul Harvey," said Irv in an interview for the book *Irv! Buffalo's Anchorman*. "Paul Harvey was not fast-paced, but he had a pace of delivering the news that was compelling. I like to think I was Paul Harvey only a lot faster."

Faster, with flagrant, more outrageous writing. In the early rock 'n' roll days of KB Radio and Pulsebeat News, the pace and the shocking style of writing and delivery made Irv's later *Eyewitness News* persona seem comatose.

Irv Weinstein, WKBW Radio News Director

"A Top-40 news guy; fast paced," said Irv. "Over time I developed a writing style that had sizzle and alliteration, and the type of thing to grab the audience. I learned along the way, that before you can get people to listen to you, you have to catch their attention. One way to do that is in your writing-- make it compelling. Sometimes it was overboard, frankly, but it was ok. It did the job."

It was the perfect comingling of man and circumstance that put Irv in the position to really invent the style of newscasting he made famous in Buffalo-- one that was copied around the country.

Henry Brach had been a drug store owner before working in radio, and there's something about that which just seems to fit. Unlike nearly every other KB Pulsebeat News man, Brach's voice didn't boom into radio speakers. His cool, understated style fit in just as well at KB, making him the favorite of listeners and a long line of America's most talented all-time disc jockeys, who were merciless in mocking the newsman.

Henry Brach in the KB studio.

Jim Fagan was a disc jockey and newsman at WBTA in Batavia, where he's shown here, before heading to WKBW for a three-decade career.

Jim Fagan's voice was one of the threads that tied together the various eras at KB. During the 27-and-a-half years that he was a newsman at WKBW Radio, he saw many come and go, but from JFK to Reagan, his was one of the voices that reported on it over KB.

His strong voice punched out the KB Pulsebeat News sound perfectly in those early years, and mellowed as the rest of the station did right up to the very end. Fagan was among the final employees when corporate owners pulled the plug on the local news and music on KB and replaced it with syndicated programming.

John Zach was born into radio. His father was a radio pioneer, having built the first "wireless set" in the city's Kaisertown neighborhood. After attending St. Casimir grammar school and PS 69, he learned about the technical aspects of radio at Seneca Vocational High School-- but John's path into broadcasting was lined with guitar pics rather than vacuum tubes.

As the leader of "John Zach and The Fury's," he played record hops with Danny Neaverth, who worked with Zach and helped him develop his on-air sound.

W.G.R. RECORD HOP featuring Daffy Dan Neaverth, John Zach and the Fury's. Cuba Central School, 8 p.m. to 11 p.m., Sat., May 9th. Admission 90c. Also free records.

1959 ad.

After spending time as a disc jockey in Georgia, Zach returned to Buffalo and was hired by Irv Weinstein for an overnight news job at WKBW in 1960. He spent most of the next five decades informing Buffalo's radio audience, *come hell or high snowbanks.* Twice during the Blizzard of '77, John Zach came in by snow mobile to anchor the news during the Danny Neaverth Show.

As KB Radio's News Director for most of the 80s, a survey found that John Zach was Buffalo's most recognizable radio news personality.

With long stops at WKBW and WGR under his belt, Zach joined WBEN in 1998 and spent 18 years with Susan Rose co-anchoring Buffalo's most listened to radio news program, Buffalo's Early News.

John Zach spent time as a disc jockey and news man in Georgia before spending nearly 27 years at WKBW Radio.

KB dominated radio in the 60s, but not morning radio.

For the fourth straight decade, Clint Buehlman was Buffalo's most listened to radio personality.

Buffalo's indestructible, omni-present, favorite uncle sometimes took his role a little too seriously--- scolding, chastising, lecturing and generally irascible.

Buehly was at his crankiest during snow storms, lashing out at those who didn't follow the rules and made things tougher for the rest of us. But with a check of "Arthur Mometer," consultation with "Mr. Operator" Tom Whalen, and a news update with Jack Ogilvie, everything seemed in order-- as that was WBEN's morning team for more than 25 years.

Whalen started on the early shift working the Buehlman show in 1948, arriving each day by 4:30 to make sure the studio was ready for Buffalo's AM-MC when his show began at 6am.

WBEN's Clint Buehlman with "Arthur Mometer."

Sometimes Clint would cut it close— especially during snow emergencies. But the plow on the front of his Jeep was usually enough to get him from Amherst to North Buffalo six days-a-week no matter the weather.

"Dependability," explained Buehly, was the reason for his 40 years of success on morning radio on WGR and then WBEN.

From the 1930s through the 1970s, if it was snowing in Buffalo on any given morning, you could depend on tuning around your dial to find "Yours Truly, Buehly" sitting at the piano, singing his song about driving in winter weather.

"Leave for work a little early cause the roads are kind of slick, and even though your brakes are good you'll find you can't stop quick.

"When you step upon that peddle and your car begins to skid, just remember this advice and you'll be glad you did."

Among those looking on as Clint Buehlman shakes hands with Erie County Executive B. John Tutuska is Ann Deckop. Deckop spent more than 55 years working at WBEN and Ch.4 as an executive assistant, community outreach coordinator, and public service director.

Charlie Bailey calls Canisius Basketball action on WEBR, assisted by Mike Donahue and engineer Ed Wheims.

Among his other duties from classical music host to newsman to call-in show moderator, Brother John Otto read children's books over WGR Sunday mornings in the early 1960s.

After nearly two decades at WEBR, Bob Wells landed at WGR Radio and TV, hosting shows on Ch.2 like Pic-A-Polka, The Yankee Doodle Room (live from AM&A's), the Money Movie, and was also the voice of Your Host Restaurants for decades.

Gene Kelly and Bernie Sandler in the new studios of WBEN-FM in 1960. WBEN-FM was Buffalo's first FM station starting in 1946. First broadcasting at 106.5FM, the station moved frequencies to 102.5FM in 1959. The following year, WBEN-FM moved into expansive new studios at 2077 Elmwood Avenue, where the station would remain until 2000, through call letter changes to WMJQ-FM and then WTSS-FM.

More listeners start tuning to FM

In 1963, Buffalo boasted 11 commercial AM stations and 11 commercial FM stations.

And by the mid-1960s, those stations on the FM dial had begun the transformation that would make *Frequency Modulation* radio's future and driving force.

The decade started with an appreciation of the calm of the FM dial.

One letter to the editor read, "Buy an F. M. (frequency modulation) radio. They don't cost much more than an ordinary A.M. set. But music comes out of an F. M. radio—not that jabberwocky they call music on A.M.

stations. Station WBNY-FM Buffalo, and WHLD-FM Niagara Falls, have good music all day long and some of the evening WBEN-FM has supper concerts. All these stations have music for the human race. No one will need a psychiatrist even after hours of listening to them."

Another Courier-Express reader wrote that he "certainly would hate to see the FM band cluttered with rock 'n' roll."

By the end of the decade, both would be terribly disheartened.

106.5FM was the longtime home of middle-of-the-road, easy listening music for two decades. WADV-FM signed on in 1962, and became the first Buffalo station to broadcast in stereo. Dan Lesniak was a WKBW Salesman when he and his wife Nancy founded the station, which they owned until 1981, when it became WYRK-FM.

WADV-FM morning man Lou German.

George "The Hound" Lorenz grew tired of working for other people, and founded WBLK-FM. The legendary Buffalo disc-jockey threw the switch to put his station on the air on Dec. 11, 1964.

ROOSEVELT TUCKER BRADLEY J. COOL JASON DENIS DON ALLEN HOUND DOG

'BLK 'FUNKY wblc 'Soul Brother,
BUFFALO FORTY' Radio' 93.7 fm

After years as chief announcer and then station manager at the old WBNY-AM, Carl Spavento was an FM pioneer. He spent nearly a decade expanding the offerings of WBUF-FM, which began broadcasting in 1947. Among his innovations: music and grocery descriptions broadcast for playback over the public address speakers at Tops Friendly Markets when the chain opened in 1962.

Along with other longtime radio veterans Ed Little and Danny McBride, Spavento was part of the team who put WBNY-FM 96.1 on the air in 1966. Operations manager Ed Little said the music fare will be "stimulating, with good taste and excitement, and the lively sounds will be transmitted with enough power to reach the entire Niagara megalopolis and nearby Canada."

Spavento later moved to WYSL as news director, before joining re-joining WBUF-FM in 1981, where he was heard reading the news on the Stan Roberts Show, among other duties over a Buffalo radio career that spanned 50 years.

WHLD-FM in Niagara Falls would eventually become WZIR and WXRT, before changing call signs to WKSE-FM, broadcasting as Kiss 98.5 since 1985.

WWOL-FM signed on in 1954 at 104.1FM. WGR signed on WGR-FM at 96.9FM in 1959, and WEBR signed on WEBR-FM at 94.5FM in 1960.

Van Miller spent the 60s as the play-by play voice of the Bills and one of Ch.4's top sportscasters, but he was also one of WBEN Radio's most popular personalities as well.

Above, Van hikes the ball to Jack Kemp. On the next page, Van interviews radio comedy legend Jack Benny and Hollywood beauty Jayne Mansfield.

346

Ch.4 had an ever-changing team of news, sports, and weather announcers.

CH 4 Highlights

NEWS-SPORTS	**WEATHER**
Chuck Healy	Tom Jolls
Reports	Early Weather
6:00-6:25 P.M.	6:25 P.M.

CBS NEWS • Walter Cronkite • 6:30 P.M.

Special—Regeneration: Buffalo Waterfront "A JEWEL FOR A CROWN?" 10:30 PM

In 1964, Tom Jolls was the weatherman on the Ch.4 newscasts anchored by Chuck Healy leading into Walter Cronkite's CBS Evening News.

Left above: Van Miller, news; Chuck Healy, sports; Ward Fenton, weather

Left below: Chuck Healy, news; Van Miller, sports, Ken Philips, weather

Ward Fenton, Bill Peters, Martha Torge, Mike Mearian, and Tom Jolls recording "The Life of FDR."

Before he made Dustmop come to life and made the phrase "Back to you, Irv," part of Buffalo's lexicon, Tom Jolls was celebrated as the host of *Kaleidoscope* on WBEN Radio. The program was filled with daily musical themes and dramatic productions often written and produced by Jolls—including the one shown above.

"I would commend Mr. Jolls for his show, its freshness, variety, presentation and the obvious effort which goes into the program. Mr. Jolls always makes Kaleidoscope sound like fun day after day," wrote one Toronto critic.

Virgil Booth, as a host and news reporter, brought nature to Ch.4 viewers.

During the station's first 11 years on the air, Chuck Poth was a familiar face to Ch.2 viewers as one of the station's most visible newscasters.

The South Buffalo native attended OLV grammar school and Baker-Victory High in Lackawanna. After serving in the Army during World War II, Poth held a string of jobs at WUSJ Lockport, WJJL Niagara Falls, WBNY, and then the short-lived WBUF-TV.

After working at WGR-TV from 1954-1966, he worked in politics, writing speeches for Robert Kennedy, then running for county legislature and congressional seats, before working in Buffalo City Hall during the Griffin administration.

By 1964, Roy Kerns (above) and Frank Dill (below) were familiar faces in Buffalo, both having been on Ch.2 since the station signed on a decade earlier. They were seen anchoring news and weather leading into NBC's Huntley/Brinkley Report.

After retiring from the Buffalo Bills, Ernie Warlick became the first Black member of a Buffalo TV anchor team when he became a sportscaster at Ch.2. While his duties generally included interviewing sports figures like Bills quarterback Tom Flores (below), they also included some news duty—like chatting with Mayor Frank Sedita during a bus strike (above).

Skating champion Peggy Fleming chats with photographers Roy Russell from The Buffalo Evening News, Don Keller (Yearke) from Ch.7, and Paul Maze from Ch.4.

The press covers the Dome Stadium controversy. At the table: reporters Jim Fagan, WKBW; Allan Bruce, UPI; Jim McLaughlin, WYSL; Milt Young, WBEN-TV, Ray Finch, WBEN-TV. Dick Teetsel, Ch.2 sits in back, and Don Yearke shoots film for Ch.7.

Irv, Rick, & Tom

Irv Weinstein used to joke that Ch.7 was the fourth station in a three-station market when he began anchoring the news there in 1964.

For most of the station's early years, there were ABC network shows and lots of old movies—and legally, not enough of anything else. In 1963, the FCC withheld the station's license renewal request "pending additional information on local, live programing" on the station.

Enter Irv.

It took a few years for the Eyewitness News approach to catch on and become number one in Buffalo, but even as early as Irv's first year at Ch.7 and a year before Tom Jolls would come over from Ch.4– the approach of dispatching news cameras to every corner of the city was gaining traction in an era where the other stations in the market were comfortable with a news anchor reading into a camera with no video or graphic accompaniment.

"They can hear about it on the other channels," said Ch.7 General Manager Robert King, "but they see it on Ch.7."

Irv Weinstein with Bill Gregory. When Irv first came to Ch.7, they co-anchored the news.

Irv Weinstein led the team that informed and entertained generations of Buffalonians with his unmistakable style in writing and delivering the news. Together with Rick Azar and Tom Jolls, Irv was a part of the longest running TV anchor team in history, and their story is the story of Buffalo over the last half century.

WKBW-TV Ch.7 signed on in 1958, 10 years after Ch.4, and four years after Ch.2, and the new station had a hard time gaining traction.

"The ratings at Ch.7 were worse than the signoff test patterns on Ch.4 and Ch.2," said Weinstein.

When Weinstein left WKBW Radio to join Ch.7 alongside Rick Azar in 1964, the evening newscast went on the air at 7:20pm to avoid competition from the other stations' 6 p.m. newscasts.

"Channel Seven News Director Irv Weinstein offers the best local coverage nightly...in air time, in film shots, and in style of delivery..."
JACK ALLEN-Buffalo Courier-Express

EYEWITNESS NEWS
7:20 P.M. 11:00 P.M. Weeknights
WKBW-TV 7

A few years later, Tom Jolls joined the crew, and the Irv, Rick and Tom team that dominated Buffalo TV news in the '70s and '80s was complete.

The three men, plus addition of more local newsfilm, better tight writing and a display of personality and human interaction unseen before on local TV made Ch.7 — and Irv Weinstein — No. 1 in the market, virtually uninterrupted, from the late 1960s through Irv's retirement in 1998.

"Basically, the other stations' approach was very conservative, you know, the globe on the desk and the clocks in the background and the mature, deep-voiced guy sitting there," explained Irv. "We were aggressive, we were razzle-dazzle. We covered every fire there was because it looked great."

Irv also credited the styles and personalities of the three men — and the mix of those personalities — with the larger success of "Eyewitness News" during those years.

Tom Jolls, 1964

"You had Tom, every mother's son; the flag, and apple pie, and all of those things that make for a fine American," said Irv. "That's what you saw, that's what you got. That's what Tom was, that's what Tom is.

"Rick was more of a broadcasting personality," said Weinstein. "Solid professional, knowledgeable, debonair, good looking guy. Very smooth, Mr. Smooth, the Latin Lover."

And rounding out the trio?

"Me? I'm an ethnic type," Irv said of himself. "Definitely an ethnic type. I felt very proud of the fact in a heavily Catholic, heavily Polish town, this Jewish kid was accepted."

357

"Accepted" is an understatement. Irv Weinstein is remembered as one of — if not the — greatest personalities in the history of Buffalo television.

He got his start in radio as a child actor growing up in Rochester in the 1940s. After working in various radio and TV jobs, he wound up as a newsman at WKBW Radio in Buffalo. There, he became the news director and was instrumental in the rock 'n' roll style newscasts that matched the music KB was playing in the late 50s and early 60s.

It was at KB Radio where Irv perfected the ra-ta-tat-tat staccato delivery style that he'd be remembered for; it's also where he developed the sharp writing style, filled with alliteration and bigger-than-life phraseology that was the engine for that delivery.

There were no firemen tamping down a house fire. "Buffalo fire eaters" "battled spectacular blazes." "Death was waiting along the side of the road" for someone struck and killed by a car. A teenage hold-up man was a "knife-wielding delinquent," if he wasn't a "pistol-packing punk."

After leaving WKBW Radio for WKBW-TV in 1964, it took Weinstein some time to get used to being on camera and to adapt his writing style for television delivery, but over the next several years, he became comfortable with TV and Buffalo became comfortable with him.

By the time Irv Weinstein came to Ch.7, Rick Azar had already been there for six years. He was the announcer who signed the station on the air in 1958.

He had been an actor who took radio jobs at WUSJ in Lockport, WWOL in Buffalo and WHLD in Niagara Falls between acting gigs, and also served as a sports and weather man on Buffalo's short lived WBUF-TV Ch.17 staring in 1956.

In the early days at Ch.7, he delivered weather, sports and news, along with general announcing, and even hosting "Buffalo Bandstand," the local version of the Dick Clark show.

It was in sports broadcasting, though, where Azar became a long-remembered and trusted household name.

As a TV sportscaster, a play-by-play man for college basketball, and one of the voices of the Buffalo Bills in the 1970s, there were few broadcasters better known, liked and appreciated that Azar.

Rick Azar in the lockerroom.

In 1975, the fact that the "Eyewitness News" anchor team might have been the hippest guys in town might be reflected in the fact that there was a special edition Oldsmobile on sale called "The Azar."

If Rick was hip, Tom Jolls was everyone's favorite neighbor. The youngest of the three, Jolls and Azar actually met when Jolls was a junior high school announcer in Lockport and Azar was a disc jockey on WUSJ using the name "Dick Corey."

Jolls eventually became the morning man at his hometown WUSJ. He also had early TV experience at another short-lived Buffalo TV station, WBES-TV. After a stint in the Army, Jolls returned to WUSJ before moving to WBEN AM-FM-TV in 1963. He was seen on Ch.4 and heard on 930AM for about two years before joining Irv Weinstein, Rick Azar and Dustmop at Ch.7 in 1965.

Commander Tom was more than just a weatherman, he was a beloved TV uncle who guided us through days that were stormy as well as salubrious, but also made sure we were entertained with the puppets he and his wife crafted from their children's old stuffed animals.

Tom Jolls on a salubrious night on the original Weather Outside set on Main Street.

But even mild-mannered Tom Jolls was a part of the spice of "Eyewitness News." For decades, it was Jolls who asked, "It's 11 o'clock. … Do you know where your children are?"

Together, the facts say that at 24 years, Irv, Rick and Tom were the longest-running anchor team in the history of American television. The hearts of Buffalonians say they were also probably the most beloved.

Rick Azar broke up the band with his retirement after 31 years at Ch.7 in 1989. The following year, at age 59, Irv Weinstein gave up the 11pm newscast and was seen only at 6pm.

He stuck around in that 6pm anchor chair for just shy of a decade, retiring from Ch.7 in 1998. Jolls followed suit with his retirement in 1999.

The Eyewitness News team included Irv Weinstein, Nolan Johannes, Barbara Pawelek, Paul Thompson, Bill Nailos, Don Keller, Alan Nesbitt, John Winston, and Tom Jolls.

Aside from Dialing For Dollars, Liz Dribben anchored morning newscasts on Ch.7 through the second half of the 1960s. Among Buffalo's first woman broadcast journalists, she became a CBS News writer and producer, working with Mike Wallace and Walter Cronkite among others.

The heavy promotion of Irv, Rick, and Tom as a team began after Ch.7's early newscasts moved to 6pm in 1971.

Cable TV comes to WNY

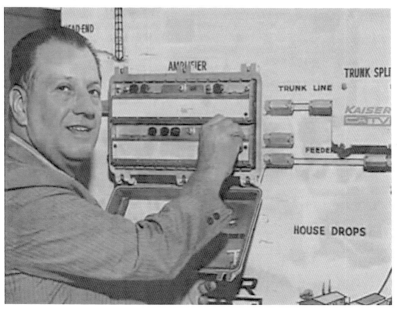

Al Anscombe at the WNY Cable TV map.

After ending the 1950s with a revolution on Buffalo radio with the switch of WKBW to rock 'n' roll Top-40, former radio announcer and longtime KB manager Alfred Anscombe had another trick up his sleeve by the mid-60s.

He was the brains and muscle behind the then-controversial idea of bringing television into Western New York homes via cable instead of antenna.

Anscombe began construction on the infrastructure which would eventually bring cable to Buffalo's northern suburbs through his Amherst Cablevision and Ken-Ton Cablevision. Both franchises were eventually sold to International Cable.

Nin Angelo spent 20 years as a professional bowler, but it was his 19-week run on Ch.4's "Beat the Champ" which made him a Buffalo pop culture icon. He not only won 19 weeks in a row, but did it in style—with a 299 game and a 760 series mixed in.

Nin Angelo, Allie Brandt, Vic Hermann—each multiple "Beat the Champ" champions, and host Chuck Healy.

Rocketship 7 & Commander Tom

Unquestionably the most popular local kids' show of the 50s and into the 60s, Uncle Mike's Playhouse on Ch.4 was Mike Mearian's lasting legacy on Buffalo media.

The 1956 Sylvania TV Award nominations described Uncle Mike this way:

"Mr. Mearian's genius as a humorist plus the best available children's cartoons add up to youthful entertainment fun that is always in the best of taste."

Uncle Mike's faithful puppet sidekick, Buttons, was a marionette operated by Ellen Knetchel and voiced by Mearian.

By the time Buttons and Uncle Mike left Buffalo for a Big Apple acting career in 1967, Buffalo rug-rats had already found fun new TV shows created just for them over on Ch.7.

Jay Nelson was a disc jockey on WKBW Radio, but is perhaps best remembered as the host of Ch.7's Jungle Jay Show.

Jungle Jay Nelson, WKBW-TV

He wore a pith helmet and a leopard print jacket while playing old Tarzan clips when kids got home from school.

The shtick was so popular that even after he left Buffalo for his native Canada to work at CHUM Radio in Toronto, he continued calling himself Jungle Jay, and continued wearing the pith helmet.

The show was just as popular north of the border as it was in Western New York, and the nickname stuck with Nelson for decades.

Sheena Queen of the Jungle (actress Irish McCalla) felt right at home on a promotional visit to Jay Nelson's Ch.7 show.

Depending on your age, you remember him best as the host of Dialing for Dollars or the host of Rocketship 7.

Mr. Beeper, Dave, and Promo

Dave Thomas spent 16 years at WKBW-TV, starting in the newsroom anchoring newscasts and weather reports. The native of Buffalo's West Side attended Holy Angels grammar school and Bishop Fallon High School.

His 16-year run on Rocketship 7-- one of the most beloved programs in the history of Buffalo television--began on September 10, 1962. Eventually Dave would be joined by the Sweetleys, Mr. Beeper and Promo the Robot.

During the show's run, there were two different Promo costumes and five different men who played him, including *Dialing For Dollars* accordion player Johnny Banaszak, who spend many years switching between his Promo and "Johnny and Jimmy" identities between shows.

Dave Thomas—real name Dave Boreanaz—left Buffalo for Philadelphia in 1978, where using the air name Dave Roberts, he was a weather man at WPVI for 31 years.

Both in Buffalo and Philadelphia, Dave was involved with the Jerry Lewis MDA Telethon, rising to National Vice Chairman.

His son is the actor Dave Boreanaz, who has played in the TV shows Buffy the Vampire Slayer, Bones, and SEAL Team.

When Dave Thomas wasn't palling around with Promo the Robot and Mr. Beeper, he was hosting Dialing for Dollars with Nolan Johannes and Liz Dribben.

Rocketship 7 was a must watch for many Buffalo kids through the 60s and 70s, before Dave Thomas blasted off for that new job in Philadelphia in 1978.

NOW, EVERY AFTERNOON TOO!

ROCKETSHIP 7

WITH

DAVE THOMAS
PROMO THE ROBOT
PAIL MAC
MR. BEEPER

TWICE A DAY
7:30 A.M. AND 4:00 P.M.

KIDS! TELL YOUR FRIENDS

This is the second paint job for the original Promo the Robot. A different costume was used in the mid-70s. John Banaszak played Promo during the part of the show's run. Each day, he quickly shed the clacking Promo suit to grab his accordion and entertain on Dialing for Dollars.

Dave Thomas and Mr. Beeper

Buffalo's longest running—and most salubrious-- kids' show starred Ch.7's All-American weatherman Tom Jolls as Commander Tom– who eventually took to TV wearing the bright red jacket of a Canadian Mountie.

He performed with his puppet pals which early on, were mostly made from his kids' old stuffed animals. Among them as voiced by the Commander himself, were Matty the Mod-- a young, energetic, but slight dimwitted alligator; the sensitive and gentle Cecily Fripple, trying to recapture her glorious past; and trusty, faithful Dustmop-- watchdog of Central Command, despite of his old age and failing eyesight.

Commander Tom's first assignment was with Bat Head, as host of "The Superman Show." Eventually, Bat Head flew back to his cave and it was just Commander Tom.

The last Ch.2 produced show which captured the imagination of the youngest viewers starred weatherman Bob Lawrence as Captain Bob. He did local cut-ins during a string of wildly different programs.

Not too long after the station signed on, he was the local host of an NBC cartoon called Colonel Bleep. After that show was canceled, he entertained kids during Ch.2's playback of old 1930s Three Stooges shorts.

Captain Bob also hosted the local presentation of The Mickey Mouse Club afternoons in the late 50s and early 60s.

Romper Room

9:00 A.M., In Color

Miss Joan presides over a TV kindergarten that will keep your tots entranced every day Monday thru Friday.

IN COLOR

Although hostess "Miss Joan" made frequent personal appearances at Buffalo-area toy stores, the Romper Room program that was broadcast on WGR-TV in the late 60s was a national version of the show, aired on dozens of stations around the country.

Puppeteer Jim Menke worked on Ch.2's Captain Bob Show as well as on WNED-TV's "Mr. Whatnot" and "Barnaby & Co." programs.

All through the 60s from Thanksgiving to Christmas, Ch.4 created holiday excitement with Bill Peters as Santa, Johnny Eisenberger as Forgetful the Elf, and Warren Jacober as Freezy the Polar Bear.

375

J. Michael Collins and Vince Saele host a WNED-TV pledge drive in the late 1960s.

Sister Mary Margaretta, Superior of St. Nicholas School, was a regular guest on Ch.4's "The Bishop Visits Your Home."

Beatlemania hits WKBW

In the simplest of terms, after decades of economic depression and war, young people of the late 1940s had less responsibility, more economic freedom and a growing segment of pop culture being cultivated to employ and take advantage of that free time and free cash.

For 70 years, more mature generations have been panning the choices of teenage girls and especially the fervor with which they make those choices.

The names change, but from Frank Sinatra to Justin Bieber, rigid-minded adults can't understand all the swooning over (some singer) with (some bizarre haircut, bizarre dance, etc.).

By 1964, American fuddy-duddies had withstood the waves of bobbysoxers and Elvis' wagging hips — but the arrival of a moppy-headed quartet of singers from England took the genre up another notch.

If there's a start date for Beatlemania, you might choose Feb. 9, 1964 — the date of the band's first appearance on "The Ed Sullivan Show." About 60 percent of American televisions were tuned to the performance of the nation's No. 1 top single, "I Want to Hold Your Hand." It aired in Buffalo on Ch.4.

Immediately, adults started to try to make sense of the mania.

In a matrix that has repeated itself time and time again as American Pop Culture has evolved, the aversion to the Beatles was just as strong as the fanaticism of their young followers.

What was it about the Beatles? everyone seemed to want to know. Was it the haircuts, asked the Courier-Express' "Enquiring Reporter" of Western New York high school students?

Lining up to get on The KB Crush Beatles Bus Caravan to Toronto

One boy from Cardinal O'Hara High School was convinced that it was "The Beatles' weird looks more than their musical ability" that made them popular. Many others agreed, but said it was the combination of talent and different looks that made the Beatles "just far out."

Whether you loved the Beatles or hated them, they were clearly a growing economic force to be reckoned with.

It wasn't just with the expected idea of record sales at places like Twin Fair, more staid institutions such as AM&A's were offering "The Beatle Bob" in their downtown and branch store beauty salons. Hengerer's was selling Beatles records and wigs.

A month after the group's first appearance on Ed Sullivan, a couple of doors down from Shea's Buffalo, the Paramount Theatre sold out a weekend's worth of closed-circuit showings of a Beatles concert.

Eighteen uniformed Buffalo Police officers were hired to help keep the peace among the more than 2,500 teens who showed up to watch the show at the Paramount, which was hosted by WKBW disc jockey Joey Reynolds. The only slight hint of misbehavior on the part of Beatles fans came when the infamous rabble-rouser Reynolds declared on the stage, "I hate the Beatles!" and he was pelted with jellybeans.

Local bands like the Buffalo Beetles, later renamed the Mods, enjoyed popularity and even their own records on the radio. After the July, 1964 release of The Beatles' first film "A Hard Day's Night," the summer of 1965 saw the release of the Beatles' second movie, "Help!," which opened at Shea's before moving onto the smaller theaters and the drive-ins.

The Beatles also played a concert at Toronto's Maple Leaf Gardens in August 1965. There were at least a couple of dozen Buffalonians in attendance courtesy of the WKBW/Orange Crush Beatles caravan, hosted by Danny Neaverth.

Danny Neaverth hosting on KB Crush Caravan to see the Beatles.

Sixteen-year-old Jay Burch of Orchard Park High School described Beatlemania from the midst of it in 1964 this way: "The Beatles' singing is OK, but it's the haircuts and dress that make them standouts. … The Beatles are different. They got a good gimmick and made it work."

John Lennon, Paul McCartney, and George Harrison of The Beatles at a Toronto press conference, speaking into a microphone from Toronto's CHUM Radio front and center.

Many of Buffalo's Beatles dreams finally came true on Oct. 22, 2015, when Paul McCartney made his first appearance in Buffalo, singing songs that many in the audience had first heard 51 ½ years earlier for the first time on a Sunday evening with Ed Sullivan.

NEMS ENTERPRISES LTD

DIRECTORS:
B. EPSTEIN · C.J. EPSTEIN · G. ELLIS · B. LEE · V. LEWIS

SUTHERLAND HOUSE, 5/6 ARGYLL STREET, LONDON, W.1

TELEPHONE: REGENT 3261
CABLES: NEMPEROR LONDON W 1

BE/jn   9th April, 1967

Arthur J. Wander, Esq.,
WOR-FM 98.7
1440 Broadway,
New York, N.Y. 10018
U.S.A.

Dear Mr. Wander,

Just a note to acknowledge your letter of the 9th ultimo which I appreciate greatly.

Whilst writing, I can now tell you that the title of the recording which I played for you when I was at the station is "A Day In The Life". This title has now been announced here as being one of the tracks for the forthcoming album.

With all best wishes.

Yours sincerely,

Brian Epstein.

Art Wander was among the first Americans to hear The Beatles' classic "A Day in the Life." Yes, that Art Wander. Long before his sports talk show days, the native of Buffalo's East Side was a national radio programmer, and hosted Beatles manager Brian Epstein in his WOR New York City office.

And . . . between the music we have the KB - VIPS.* You know them all! Join the "in group" and go-go nightly . . . follow the VIPS on WKBW. .

*VIP'S
JEFFERSON KAYE
FRED KLESTINE
DAN NEAVERTH
ROD RODDY
STAN ROBERTS
LEE VOGEL

WKBW
RADIO 1520 ON YOUR DIAL
A CAPITAL CITIES STATION

The KB mid-60s lineup included midday man Rod Roddy, who would later be one of the country's leading game show announcers on shows like Press Your Luck and The Price is Right.

THE KB KLASSICS

1968

WKBW'S ALL-TIME TOP 300

The KB BUNCH

buffalo

*In the late 60s, KB issued two different top 300 lists. The band members
are the KB disc jockeys shown on the previous page, with the exception of
Lee Vogel—who had left the station, and was shown facing backwards.*

Ramblin' Lou & the Family Band

"The big man with the gentle voice and the white Stetson."

There's no doubt who Buffalo News reporter Dan Herbeck was describing-
- but Buffalo's pioneer of country music, Ramblin' Lou Schriver. He's
performed at the Grand Ole Opry and he and his wife Joanie Marshall are
in the Country Music Hall of Fame. But it all started much more simply
than that.

As a senior at Tonawanda High,
Lou Schriver walked into the
brand new WJJL Radio in the
Elks Building in Niagara Falls
and asked for an on-air try-out.

The station manager liked the
sound, and offered Lou the
chance at a daily, unpaid show.

He was driving his 1933 Ford to
the station every day before
school for a 15-minute program
of "hillbilly music," and it caught
on.

Ramblin' Lou for Milk for Health

"When I started, country music was not the thing. In the early days, more
people ridiculed it," said Schriver in 1978. "But I was very proud to be
called country."

The grandson of "an old-time Pennsylvania fiddler who rode through the
hills looking for dances to play," Lou spent the next 17 years on the radio
in Niagara Falls, and building an audience for country music all across
Western New York.

"I love the music. I love the people who love the music. The kind of people
who like country music are down-to-earth. There's nothing put-on about

them," said Lou, who came to Buffalo in 1964 to help build a country sound for WWOL Radio as the station's program director.

Joanie Marshall, also known as Mrs. Lou Schriver, grew up in Cheektowaga—but she, too, is all country. She was nine months pregnant when she played her double-necked electric guitar with Buck Owens when the country legend played on a Buffalo stage.

She felt a little woozy during the show, but glowed in the big applause from the audience and praise from Owens on the stage.

Only hours later, Ramblin' Lou rushed his wife to the hospital, and Lou Jr. was born.

The Schrivers have always made their music and their business a family affair. Early on, the band included Lou, Joanie, Joanie's dad "Bashful Eddie" Marshall on the bass, legendary side man "Accordion Zeke" Cory, Don Atkinson on drums and Bill Dyet on the steel guitar. They played gigs around the region together, and also on "The WGR Jamboree" on Ch.2.

In 1970, the Schrivers bought WMMJ Radio from Stan Jasinski, who was selling the station he built on William Street in Lancaster to pour his resources into the television station he was starting, WUTV-TV Ch.29.

Among the radio station's first employees was Accordion Zeke—who became a WXRL Account Executive.

Lou Jr. eventually joined the "family band" on drums. Daughter Lori Ann plays the fiddle, and Lynn Carol Schriver sings and plays electric piano. Through the 80s, Linda Lou was the receptionist at WXRL and a featured singer in the family band. She started singing with the band at age 4 on Ch.2, and at 13 replaced her grandpa on the bass in the band.

"The family that plays together, stays together," said Lou, who always treated everyone like family, and had associations that stretch more than

four decades with The Erie County Fair, Milk for Health, Tops, and a host of other sponsors.

The Schrivers at WXRL, 1970.

Dialing for Dollars

"A lot of friendliness and little schmaltz seem to work just fine for 'Dialing for Dollars'," wrote Buffalo Evening News Critic Gary Deeb in 1971, by which time, the show had already been a mid-morning mainstay on Ch.7 for seven years.

Nolan Johannes came to WKBW-TV in May 1964 — and by the end of the year, was the permanent host of the brand new "Dialing for Dollars." His first co-host was Liz Dribben, who left Ch.7, eventually joining CBS in New York as a writer  and producer for such luminaries as Walter Cronkite, Mike Wallace, Charles Osgood and Dan Rather.

387

Lafayette High and UB grad Liz Dribben left Ch.7 in 1969 after being refused pay equity with her male counterparts at the station.

Aside from phone calls trying to give away money, the show was filled with interviews of the everyday women in the audience, twice-weekly exercise tips from UB's Dr. Len Serfustini, syndicated features from "The Galloping Gourmet" Graham Kerr and "Fashions in Sewing" with Lucille Rivers.

Liz Dribben and Phyllis Diller, wearing Bills clothes and doing a workout routine on "Dialing for Dollars."

The half-hour show grew to 90 minutes, and in 1969, weatherman and "Rocketship 7" host Dave Thomas joined Johannes as co-host.

And even decades after the show went off the air, most Buffalonians of a certain age will be able to recall without hesitation the names of the guys in the "Dialing for Dollars" band — Jimmy and Johnny.

In 1978, Thomas left Ch.7 for Philadelphia, and "Dialing for Dollars" was reformatted to become "AM Buffalo." Johannes left Ch.7 in 1983 to become a news anchor in Scranton, Pa.

Jimmy Edwin, drums, and Johnny Banaszak, accordion, on the set of Dialing for Dollars. Banaszak was also one of the men who wore the Promo the Robot costume on Rocketship 7 through the years.

Nolan Johannes on the set of Dialing for Dollars, inside WKBW-TV s Main Street studios.

Broadcasting live from the Erie County Fair is a tradition that dates back to the earliest days of TV in Buffalo, and Meet the Millers—starring turkey farmers Bill and Mildred Miller—were regulars at the fair all through the 50s and 60s. They're shown here with another Ch.4 personality ready to broadcast live from Hamburg—John Corbett (left).

WKBW-TV's broadcast license renewal was held up in the early 60s for a lack of quality local programming, but fans of campy old monster movies didn't mind. Films like Frankenstein Meets the Wolfman were regular fare on Ch.7—and a generation later helped spark *Off Beat Cinema*'s quirky tribute to the genre on the station.

In 1968, WGR-TV's new news team included George Redpath, Pat Fagan, Doris Jones, and Frank Benny.

BUFFALO'S 1st Two-Man NEWS TEAM

Now Brings You Local News Film in Color

ANOTHER 1st ON

By the end of the 60s, WGR-TV's anchor team had changed again—this time with Henry Marcotte (above) with news, Mike Nolan (below) with sports, and Frank Benny—who had been on the sports desk—moved over to the weather map. Marcotte didn't hide his conservative views-- which made him the target of protesting UB students and striking NABET members who watched him cross their picket lines. Replaced by Ron Hunter, Marcotte went on to work as an editorial writer and booth announcer for NBC in New York City.

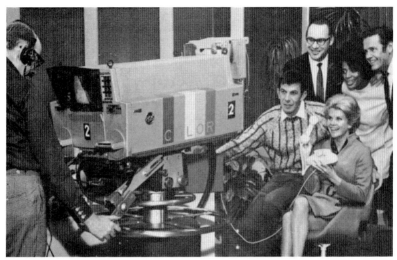

Star Trek's Leonard Nimoy, R&B singer Ruth McFadden, actress Barbara Anderson, "You Asked for It" host Jack Smith, and telethon chairman Michael Allis in the Ch.7 studios.

Gov. Nelson Rockefeller visits with Irv Weinstein at Ch.7's Main Street studios.

The media gathers for Jack Kemp's 1969 announcement that he's retiring from football and running for Congress. That's Ch.4's Ray Finch, Ch.4's Paul Maze, Ch.7's Sam Brunetta with handheld camera, Ch.4's Virgil Booth, Larry Felser, Ch.4's Len Johnson on audio, Ch.7's John Winston, Ch.4's Van Miller, Jack Kemp, and Ch.7's Rick Azar.

Ch.4 photojournalist Bill Cantwell got mixed up in the action covering Buffalo's civil rights protests of 1967. Cantwell was best known over his long career for his serene nature shots used during Ch.4's weather segments.

TV news gathering and video recording technology rapidly evolved in the 60s. News editor John Kreiger (left) is writing copy from film shot by Mike Mombrea, Sr. (right) and edited by Quint Renner (center). Mombrea spent 32 years as a photojournalist at Ch.4, starting as a true pioneer—a TV news cameraman in the days when TV was just starting. It was through Mike's viewfinder that Western New York witnessed the Attica Prison uprising, the installation of Pope John Paul II, and somewhere north of one million feet of news film capturing the day-to-day happenings of Western New York.

Recording video tape in the field for news purposes was still a decade away, but by Ch.4's 20th anniversary in 1968, the station had three color video tape machines.

Engineers Frank Maser, Ralph Voigt, and Edgar Steeb with VTRs.

In 1969, WBEN-TV revamped its news format, calling their newscasts "First Team News."

A deluge of print ads showed the team in action, including news anchor Chuck Healy, reporting from the dewatered Niagara Falls alongside the WBEN-TV News mobile unit, Van Miller from Bills practice with-- among others-- Number 40 Ed Rutkowski looking on, and weather man Ken Philips in studio in front of his maps.

WBEN also very heavily promoted the broadcasts of Buffalo Bills Football with Van Miller, Stan Barron, and Dick Rifenburg.

In the booth at the Rockpile: Linda Arnold, Herm Brunotte, Willard
Fredericks, Jim Georgeson, Bruce Wexler. Murray Wilkinson, Dick
Rifenburg, Stan Barron, Van Miller, Tony Vacanti

The WBEN Bills Team: Bruce Wexler, Dr. Ed Gicewicz, Art Graff, Dick
Rifenburg, Ray Sinclair, Willard Fredericks, Van Miller, Jim Georgeson,
Stan Barron, Bob Werner, Linda Arnold, Herm Brunotte, and Tony
Vacanti

Through the 50s and 60s, WBEN AM-FM-TV was thought of as a single unit, The Buffalo Evening News Stations. Talent and technicians often moved between the stations to where they were needed, and the product in each place was reflective of each other.

In 1968, when Phil "Bucky" Buchanan and John Eaton *(left)* would arrive at WBEN around 4am to begin writing news for Jack Ogilvie, the most you'd hear from them is a mention from Jack about who was sitting at the Editor's desk.

Soon thereafter, news gathering operations for WBEN Radio and Ch.4 were made independent for the first time. The newsrooms were at opposite ends of the same hall at 2077 Elmwood Avenue, and information was freely shared— but editorial decisions and staff were structurally separated. Five full-time writers and a news director were assigned to WBEN Radio, as separating the newsrooms allowed for a change in union rules which barred writers from reporting on air, and announcers from writing.

One immediate change was to hear the voices of long-time "news editors" Marty Gleason and Fran Lucca on the air at WBEN, after the two men had spent decades writing scripts for Ogilvie, Lou Douglas, Ward Fenton, and others to read.

Marty Gleason, right, at the editor's desk

Fran Lucca spent more than 60 years in Buffalo media, starting with a column he wrote for the Buffalo Evening News as a Boy Scout in 1939. After returning from active duty in the Navy following World War II, Lucca spent 23 years at WBEN AM-FM-TV as a writer, reporter, and producer, and then another 14 years at WNED-TV creating documentary-style reports on local subjects for Ch.17.

Fran Lucca takes a quick smoke break in the WBEN-TV newsroom.

The change went both ways. Some longtime news "announcers" couldn't handle the role of journalist.

Longtime announcer Lou Douglas loved it.

The Korean War vet came to WBEN-AM/FM/TV in 1957 and his unflappable, smart, level-headed approach to news anchoring and interviewing was part of the fabric of the station for 30 years.

In his early years as a junior announcer at The Buffalo Evening News stations, television still played second fiddle to AM radio. Many of his early assignments were on Ch.4, including regular 6pm walks from WBEN's Statler studios to The Buffalo Evening News' building near the foot of Main Street. He'd read-- as announced at the beginning of each newscast, "From the Editorial Floor of the Buffalo Evening News" -- the 6 o'clock television news as prepared by the newspaper staff.

Douglas would continue to appear as a reporter, host, and announcer on TV through the 1970s, but he is best remembered for his work at WBEN Radio. It was his voice that anchored radio coverage of President John F. Kennedy's visit to Buffalo in 1962. He broadcast from inside the prison complex during the Attica uprising over WBEN Radio, as well.

Living in Kenmore, his home was closest to the WBEN's Elmwood Avenue studios– which meant extended duty for Lou during the Blizzard of 1977.

In spanning three decades, Douglas really had two separate careers at WBEN-- one as a staff announcer, and one as a journalist. He was one of the few to excel at both.

As civil unrest and student protests rocked the UB campus through the late 60s and early 70s, WBEN's Lou Douglas (standing) was one of the voices of reason, using his evening news interview program to bring together school administrators and dissident students.

Al Fox brought humor and insight to the WBEN Farm Report show, which he hosted during the 5am hour on WBEN for 28 years, starting in 1947.

"I learned that you've got to spend time with the farmers to know what they are thinking," he said in 1961. "Only then can you provide them with the kind of program they want and need."

Ground up by radio: Bill Masters & Frank Benny

Known as *Mr. Warmth*, Bill Masters had feet planted in two different worlds. He hosted middays on WBEN through the 60s and 70s, but "understood" what was going on elsewhere in the culture and on the radio dial—He was one of the guys at the Babcock Boys' Club with Danny Neaverth and Joey Reynolds.

Maybe he'd say something outrageous, but it was hard to notice, blending in with the calm, homespun, *aw shucks* delivery that made him a great fit on WBEN.

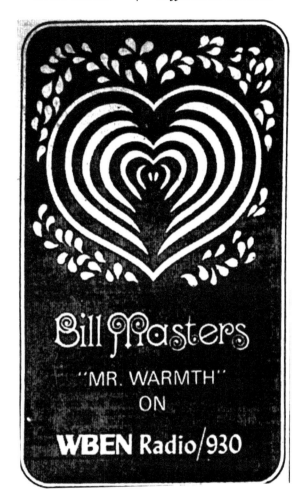

"He was known for his acerbic wit, rebellious stands and wild, unpredictable personality," wrote News reporter Anthony Violanti in 1989.

But Masters' world fell apart in 1975 when he suffered a nervous breakdown. Losing his high-profile WBEN job and his family, Masters would spend the next couple decades bouncing between radio jobs and the welfare rolls.

"Radio is a terrible f------ business," Masters told Violanti. "When you are a radio personality, every day of your life you give your pound of flesh. Sometimes, you never get it back."

Frank Benny was Buffalo radio's "master of the one-liners." He could fire them off as fast as Carson.

But that's not necessarily what people think of when they hear his name.

Frank Benny's story was called "the most outstanding comeback in the history of Buffalo broadcasting" by News critic Gary Deeb. Nearly half a century later, that record appears to be intact.

Benny was a constant on Buffalo radio dials for 25 years. His voice and style were smooth and sonorous. He quickly became Buffalo's definitive warm, friendly announcer upon coming to WGR Radio in 1965. By 1968, he was a regular on Ch.2 as well, first on the sports desk, and then for nearly a decade as the station's main weather anchor at 6 and 11.

By 1970, he was one of Buffalo's most in-demand announcers. He told The News he was generally working on about four hours of sleep. His day started as WGR Radio's morning man, then he hosted WGR-TV's Bowling for Dollars and Payday Playhouse 4 o'clock movie, and he did the weather forecasts on Ch.2. He was the NBA Buffalo Braves' first PA announcer in the 1970-71 season.

In five years at WGR, he became one of Buffalo's most popular media personalities. That was helpful in identifying him the day he robbed a bank on his way home from the radio station in June 1971.

A holdup of the Homestead Savings and Loan at the corner of Main and Chateau Terrace in Snyder netted $503 for a man wearing a stocking over his head and brandishing a (later-found-to-be toy) gun.

Minutes later, Amherst Police were arresting Benny at gunpoint in the driveway of his Williamsville home.

Frank Benny, Ch.2 sports, late 60s

The case was a local sensation. Management at WGR and at least three other stations ordered that the on-air staff not make any snide remarks or jokes at Benny's expense.

One notable exception was Ch.7, where the 6 p.m. "Eyewitness News Reel" featured the title card "Forecast: Cloudy" for the otherwise-straight Benny story. At 11, the title was changed to "Under the Weather."

The disc jockey, TV weather man and father of two was charged with third-degree robbery and was tried in a non-jury trial. The prosecution rested when Benny's attorney agreed to the facts of the case — that the announcer had indeed stuck-up the bank — but that he was innocent of the charges in the "poorly planned, ludicrous robbery" because he was temporarily insane.

Four psychiatrists testified that Benny was "not in sufficient possession of his faculties at the time of the holdup." A Buffalo General psychiatrist who had examined Benny said that the temporary mental illness was caused by extreme and prolonged stress.

First, Benny was a central figure in a protracted labor strike at WGR AM-FM-TV. Eighty members of NABET, the union representing nearly all the operations personnel and announcers at WGR, spent nine months on strike. About 10 — including Benny — crossed picket lines to continue to work. Station management provided Benny an armed guard after rocks were thrown through the windows of his home and his family was threatened.

Benny's family was also threatened the very morning of the robbery. He'd racked up thousands of dollars of gambling debts, and the bookmakers were calling in their markers — or else.

In October 1971, the judge found Benny not guilty by reason of mental disease, and he was ordered to spend two weeks at Buffalo State Hospital.

Frank Benny in the WGR Radio studio.

Then, in December, within six months of the robbery, Benny was back on WGR Radio and TV. Having been found not guilty, and "on a wave of public sympathy," management thought it was the right thing to do.

"A lot of people have told me that it takes guts to do this, to go back on the air," Benny told The News during his first week back at WGR. "But to me, it's not a courageous thing. It's a simple case of going back to what I know."

That's not to say that Benny wasn't thankful.

"It's hard to fathom that people can be that nice," Benny told News critic Deeb. "It's nice to know people can be forgiven."

All told, Benny spent 19 years at WGR, walking away from the station in 1985. For a year-and-a-half, he was the morning man at WYRK Radio, before finishing out the '80s as a weekend staffer at WBEN.

No matter what his personal life sounded like, he always sounded like Frank Benny on the radio. After leaving WBEN Radio in 1989, Benny left for Florida, where he was on the radio for 16 years — until he died in 2005 at age 67.

Frank Benny congratulates a WGR Hi-Lo Loser-Winner.

*Two completely different looking AM Radio airstaffs of the late 60s.
WBEN's Christmas carolers are Bill Masters, John Corbett, Clint
Buehlman, Ken Philips, Gene Kelly, and Al Fox. Van Miller, Stan Barron,
Jack Ogilvie, and John Luther.*

*WYSL's air staff was not quite as clean-cut. Standing outside the station's
425 Franklin Street studios are Jack Evans, Roger Christian, Jack
Sheridan, Michael O'Shea (Howard Lapidis), and Jim Bradley (Jerry Reo).
Kneeling: Rufus Coyote (Lee Poole), Kevin O'Connell, Mike Butts, and
George Hamberger.*

From the back of the WYSL XXI Boss Oldies album, with Beethoven wearing sunglasses on the cover. Second from the left, Gary Byrd, went onto a ground breaking career in New York City.

Bishop Timon grad George Hamberger and Bennett grad Kevin O'Connell both enjoyed long careers in broadcasting. Hamberger was WGR's morning man in the 80s. O'Connell worked at Ch.4 before heading to Los Angeles for the early 80s. He spent 25 years as Ch.2's main weather anchor.

413

WGR Radio News Minutemen, 1961

On the radio, on the telephone: John Otto

"I try to skewer with grace. I love being called a curmudgeon."

John Otto may have been Buffalo's greatest curmudgeon. Scholarly and erudite, but with a playful silly streak that kept listeners glued to his "conference call of all interested parties" for nearly 40 years.

He spent the 50s and early 60s doing just about everything imaginable on-air— and doing it superbly, first on WBNY and then on WGR, both radio and TV.

He was a classical music host, radio news anchor, and TV weatherman-- but he seemed best in his element once he began hosting talk shows, specifically WGR Radio's "Expression," a nightly moonlit program which invited "listeners to telephone spontaneous, unrehearsed opinions" starting in 1962.

Such would be Otto's gig, more or less, for the next 37 years.

John Otto invites listeners to telephone spontaneous, unrehearsed EXPRESSION with their opinions on subjects of current interest / Monday thru Friday / 10 PM to 12 Midnight / EXPRESSION is another important aspect of WGR's new FULL RANGE PROGRAMMING /

WGR "PUSH BUTTON ONE" 550 ON YOUR RADIO DIAL

A TRANSCONTINENT RADIO STATION

"He's a good show with his deep, pulpit-shaped voice because his unshakeable confidence forces you take sides," wrote News Radio Critic Hal Crowther in 1973. "If you agree with him, it's 'Give 'em hell, John,' but if you're against him you're often sorry that there are six or seven miles of night between your fingers and his windpipe."

"Dracula and I have a lot in common," Otto told News reporter Mary Ann Lauricella in 1981. "Daylight rather frightens us back into our caves. My metabolism is so attuned to nighttime hours that I'm more comfortable at night, when a velvet cloak is wrapped around the world."

"He takes delight in practicing conversation as an art," wrote Lauricella. "He uses a metaphor here, a simile there, perhaps a humorous play on words and weaves them into bright conversational tapestries."

But Otto preferred self-depreciation to plaudits.

"I'm certainly not modern in anything— from the way I dress to the way I think," said Otto in 1978, who was still dressing in "outdated narrow ties and straight-legged pants."

"Weekends, I tend to fall out in customary corduroy slacks and white socks. I even let myself go a day without shaving. It's a very exciting life I lead," Buffalo's congenial co-communicator told News reporter Jane Kwiatkowski in 1986.

His biggest vice, Otto confided nightly to his listeners, was his "regular investment of fortunes at Hamburg or Batavia." Otto loved the horses, and would announce the winners from the local tracks on his show.

"We have the first three from Batavia Downs," he'd say, often with commentary on the horse's name, but sometimes with the hint of disdain in his voice. "It's the rental of a horse for two minutes to run across the finish line first, and they seldom do," said Otto of his horsing around.

Catching him in a moment of serious self-reflection, it was clear Otto had loftier goals for his nightly meeting of the minds. "If it works right, it raises the level of community thought and sets people to thinking with some added knowledge they didn't have before."

"We want to occupy and engage thoughts and to allow the opportunity for people to have access to a forum they are otherwise denied," said Otto. "Some people call in who are just passing through and want to say 'hi' to the world—to let others know they are alive—a fact sometimes overlooked by the rest of the world."

Not every caller "wants to unburden himself on the big hot-line issues like Vietnam, Watergate, crime in the streets, drugs, and the rest." Otto's often hardboiled entrenchment on those issues easily and often made way for the kind of calls an overnight program attracts.

"We get a lot of older people, lonely people. What they need are some voices in the night. And they have other things on their minds besides the headlines," said Otto.

"One thing I've learned on this show is that many of them have an abiding fascination for marvels. Anything about the supernatural, ESP, UFOs, and

experience that can't be explained—that will get them talking like nothing else."

For decades, Otto was ol'trusty—the iron horse of radio. Starting in 1955, through his first 30 years in broadcasting, he never missed a day of work—not once called in sick.

John Otto, 1962

However, he landed in the hospital in 1985 with pneumonia. "Forty years of smoking," he said. The streak was broken and over the next decade and a half, sickness in breathing would slowly take Otto's life— right before your listenership's ears.

Eventually, very labored breathing made it difficult for him to get around, and he spent his final year "on the radio, on the telephone" broadcasting from his home. Even in his final days, "John, John, your operator on," didn't miss a broadcast. He signed off with his signature "I'll be with you" on a Friday, went to the hospital on Saturday, and died early Monday. He was 70 when he died in 1999.

Jim Santella's presence and sensibility blazed the trail for progressive rock radio in Buffalo, starting at WBFO (above), then notably at WGRQ and WUWU. Santella's on-air presence mellowed in the 90s in a return to WBFO as a blues host and the original co-host of Theater Talk with Anthony Chase. His 2015 book, "Classic Rock, Classic Jock" was itself an instant classic, with an in-depth look back at one of the great eras in Buffalo radio.

How to talk to your kid, the Hippie

BREAD, GOLD	Money
IT'S NOT MY BAG	Not for me
NITTY GRITTY	Down to brass tacks
SOCK IT TO ME	Give it to me straight
UP TIGHT	Nervous, insecure
WHERE IT'S AT	How things are

A Public Service Message for Parents

brought to you by

WKBW Radio
1520

on everybody's dial

This ad from a 1967 Buffalo Hockey Bisons program explained some of the far-out jive coming from America's youth. It was clearly meant as a joke, but probably actually provided insight to more than one dad, sitting in the gray seats at the Aud, flipping through the program to find a Hershey Bears or Cleveland Barons roster.

Lifelong Lockport resident Hank Nevins has been heard up and down Buffalo's radio dial for more than 40 years, but his career began overseas.

He volunteered to head to Vietnam the day after he graduated from broadcasting school, and was heard on American Forces Vietnam Network in starting in 1969.

In Southeast Asia, he worked with, among others, Pat Sajak.

Since returning home, Nevins worked as a disc jockey, host, and manager at radio stations in Western New York nearly without pause. Most recently, he's spent more than a dozen years as the Saturday morning host on WBEN.

Dennis Majewicz was both Mac McGuire and Mike Melody at WNIA in the late 60s. He went onto a long career in broadcast engineering at Ch.4, Empire Sports Network, and now back at 1230am.

The deejay's names never changed at WNIA, neither did the fact that Richard Maltby's Midnight Mood would play every night at midnight. To put it mildly, WNIA was a quirky station. The daily noon time Catholic prayers were bookended by rock 'n' roll music.

There was also the reminder to be big, be a builder. The minute-long, run-on diatribe was the brainchild of station owner Gordon Brown in reaction to the war protests of the late 60s.

The impression your friends and others have of you is based on what you do-- to teach, to create, to accomplish, or to build, whether you dig the trench for the foundation for a building; whether you lay the last brick on its top; whether you work with a pick and shovel or with the tools and machines, or in the office, or sell the products or services of industry; whether you grow, prepare or harvest the very food we eat, whether you are a homebuilder raising, teaching or educating your family or others how to become a builder, no matter what you are or what you do, if you are a builder, you are one to be long remembered.

Those who attempted to destroy the pyramids of Egypt were despised and soon forgotten, those thousands who labored to build them will never be forgotten. Be big, Be a builder.

Muhammad Ali in the WBEN studios with "Viewpoint" host Garfield Hinton.

Vice President Hubert Humphrey makes a Presidential campaign swing through Western New York in 1968, with KB newsman Jim Fagan over his shoulder holding up the microphone. Next to Jim is Buffalo Congressman Thaddeus Dulski. Over Humphrey's other shoulder is Erie County Democratic Chairman Joe Crangle.

Jeff Kaye & KB's War of the Worlds

Jeff Kaye might be best remembered by his rich, well-controlled voice and his ability to use it. He came to Buffalo as a rock 'n' roll disc jockey in 1966, but very quickly was tapped for more substantial duties.

As program director at WKBW Radio through the late 60s and early 70s, his voice was the station's anchor. Later, that voice brought an even-greater sense of gravitas to WBEN where did the impossible, replacing Clint Buehlman in 1977. Eventually, he became the voice of NFL Films and the sound that a generation of football fanatics would associate with those highly-produced highlights packages.

That all-time "voice of God" wasn't even Kaye's greatest asset. His ability to turn the fantasy in his head into great radio copy and superbly produced radio elements made him an all-time create force in the history of broadcasting.

His reboot of War of the Worlds on KB, first airing Halloween Night 1968, was an instant classic-- impeccably conceived, produced, and promoted.

Monday - Letter received from WKBW!!! WKBW plans to air H.G. Welles' "War of the Worlds" starting at 11:00 p.m., Halloween night. WKBW REQUESTED OUR CO-OPERATION IN PUBLICITY SO THAT THERE WILL BE NO PANIC.

The masterful promotional folks at KB knew that by sending out this warning–with hope of it being published, that people would flock to hear-- as Jeff Kaye puts it in the intro to the 1971 version of the dramatization-- "what all the hubhub was about."

As a producer and programmer, Kaye found superb vehicles not only for his own vocal talent, but also put the stars of KB in situations where they could shine brightest. The writing and production on a piece like "War of the Worlds" stands up 50 years later, and gives the listener a true sense of the talent that went into "playing the hits" on KB.

Three different versions of the War of the Worlds ran on KB. The primary

OUR LEADER

Jeffrey Kaye

JK-1

difference in each is the news, the deejay and the music at the start of the show. Sandy Beach was in the original broadcast in 1968, Jack Armstrong was in the 1971 version, and Shane in 1973.

In 1974, Jeff Kaye became the afternoon drive host on KB's competitor WBEN, effectively ending any future reworking of the "covering of the invasion" half of the show–which remained mostly unchanged through the different broadcasts.

Membership card showing Jeff Kaye, leader of KB's Teenage Underground.

Sandy Beach starts his 52-year run in Buffalo Radio

His famous laugh filled Buffalo airwaves for more than 50 years, and the jingle that opened his WBEN talk show for 23 of those years says Sandy Beach is "bigger than life and twice as loud."

Sandy Beach, inside the KB studio

That may be, but News critic Jeff Simon added this in 2007:

Sandy Beach "may be the most talented figure in (the) storied history of Buffalo radio," and Beach was the "last legend still heard daily on Buffalo radio."

Aside from a brief stop in Erie, Pennsylvania and four years in Milwaukee, Beach has been a constant in Buffalo radio since arriving at WKBW to take over the night shift there in 1968.

Listening to even five minutes of his show – any of his shows – over the course of 52 years is explanation enough for why News critic Hal Crowther dubbed Beach "the Needle" shortly after the deejay landed on the Buffalo radio scene.

In a 1972 interview, legendary WKBW Program Director Jeff Kaye said that within four years of arriving in Buffalo, Sandy had "worked every shift on KB except morning drive, and improved the ratings in each part."

Beach spent the 70s, 80s and 90s in and out of Buffalo as a disc jockey, program director and eventually a talk show host. After leaving his post as KB Radio's Program Director in the early 80s, he held morning show jobs at Buffalo's Hot 104 and then Majic 102.

He hosted talk shows on WBEN and WGR before leaving town for the mid-90s, but when he came back to host afternoons on WBEN in 1997, he was ready to make the change permanent.

"I liked playing the oldies," Sandy said coming back, "but you can only play 'Doo-Wap-Diddy' so many times."

Six years later, he would play oldies once again, this time at WBEN's sister station and his old stomping grounds, now sporting the call letters WWKB. For the three years KB played music of the 50s and 60s from 2003-06, Beach was a disc jockey mid-mornings and a talk show host for afternoon drive on WBEN.

The show was never edgy or provocative just for the sake of being so—but

Beach was strong in proclaiming his often-conservative views and left little room for opinions (or leaders) he thought were weak or unfounded.

Stan Roberts, Dan Neaverth, Sandy Beach. Late 60s.

When he left WBEN in 2020, management called Beach a "provocative and edgy talk show host" who entertained with "distinct humor." And an unforgettable laugh.

Watching TV rarely gets you on the front page of the paper, but it seems appropriate that it did for the staff at Tonawanda's Jenss Twin-Ton Department store in 1969.

That man would step foot on the moon is an unimaginable, superlative, epoch-defining feat in human history. But that more than half a billion would watch it happen live on their television sets made it a definitive moment in a broadcast television industry that was barely 20 years old at the time.

Gathered around the TV "to catch a few glimpses of the Apollo 11 events" were Mrs. James Tait, Margaret Robinson, Marian Feldt, Jack Dautch, Grace Hughes, Dorothy Wiegand, Rose Sugden and Rose Ann Fiala.

By the time of the 1969 moon landing, Jenss Twin-Ton's future was already in doubt as city fathers in the Tonawandas were looking to expand already present Urban Renewal efforts to include the store at Main and Niagara. Jenss Twin-Ton closed in 1976 when the building was bulldozed as urban renewal caught up.

Thanks for joining me on this look back through the early years of radio and TV in Buffalo.

The examination of history doesn't end when the book goes to press...in fact, I've found quite the opposite to be true.

And remember—work on 1970-present is already in the works.

Please help make any future volumes more rich, full, and vibrant with your stories and images.

Please reach out with additional photos, audio, video, and ephemera to steve@buffalostories.com

And be sure to check out buffalostories.com for more of Buffalo's pop culture history.

-Steve Cichon, August 2020

Thanks...

Uncle Bob Cohen, my first radio mentor

Kevin Keenan, my second radio mentor, who gave me my first job and introduced me to my wife

My wife, Monica, who I met through the window of the WBEN newsbooth early one cold Sunday morning in 1993, when she came in to deliver a 5am newscast while I was running the board. Aside from being the love of my life, she also edited this book.

Ed Little, John Demerle, and Al Wallack are only three of the dozens and dozens of amazing people who took me under their wing and taught me the crafts of radio and journalism. And life.

Jarin Cohen and Marty Biniasz are two radio pals who are true brothers. My story is inseparable from theirs, and these stories are their stories, too.

Marty Biniasz, Jack Tapson, Dan Neaverth, Mike Beato, Bob Collignon, Jay Lauder, Walt Haefner, John Bisci, Scott Fybush, and dozens more have all shared items that have become a part of this work.

If nothing else, this book proves that newspaper writers craft the first draft of history.

Bits and pieces of biographical and factual data in this volume have been pulled from thousands and thousands of newspaper articles collected and read through the years.

Hundreds of writers and editors have had a hand in crafting those pieces, and I thank them all. But most notably, I'd like to thank the men and women who have either been on the broadcasting beat or have somehow made radio and tv something they've written about in the Courier-Express and The Buffalo News with regularity, among them, in no particular order:

Jeff Simon, Gary Deeb, Hal Crowther, Lauri Githens, Jack Allen, Anthony Violanti, Mary Ann Lauricella, Alan Pergament, Mary Kunz Goldman, J. Don Schlaerth, Don Trantor, Jim Trantor, Jane Kwiatkowski, Jim Baker, Scott Thomas, Sturgis Hedrick, Doug Smith, Margaret Sullivan, Rose Ciotta, and dozens of others.

About Steve Cichon

Author Steve Cichon is an award-winning writer and radio newsman who has spent the last three decades telling the story of Buffalo, *one story at a time.*

As a teenager, he wrote and produced news and sports programming on WBEN and served as gameday producer for Buffalo Bills Football. Later, he served as Executive Producer of the Sabres Radio Network.

His first shot in front of the microphone came again as a teen, this time high above Western New York's highways as WBEN's airborne traffic reporter. He was host of newsmagazine "Buffalo's Evening News," and an overnight night talk show host during the October Surprise storm.

For a decade, Cichon's primary job was news anchor and reporter at WBEN Radio, covering courts, the Town of Amherst, the City of Buffalo, Hurricane Katrina, the crash of Flight 3407 and Presidential visits—but the beat that meant the most was the one he created for himself, that is, working to capture the essence of Buffalo in all of his reporting.

Even with "a face for radio," Cichon worked in television as a producer at Ch.4, helped create and produce the "radio on TV" Simoncast with Howard Simon on Empire Sports Network and 107-7 WNSA, and was a producer on a PBS-WNED documentary on America's opioid crisis.

Twice Steve has served in management roles in broadcasting. As a 24-year old, he was named Program Director of Buffalo sports talker WNSA Radio. He also proudly served as WBEN Radio News Director.

The author of six books dealing with various aspects of Buffalo's history, Cichon has also written more than 1,700 articles for The Buffalo News on Western New York's pop culture history, including his popular "Torn-down Tuesday" feature.

His work as a broadcast journalist has been recognized with more than two dozen Associated Press Awards AP for general excellence, use of medium, spot news coverage and enterprise reporting. Cichon has also been named Buffalo Spree's Best of Buffalo Blogger of the Year, an Am-Pol Citizen of the Year, Medaille College's Radio News Director of the Year, and was a Business First 40 Under 40 selection.

More than anything else, Steve's a Buffalonian who worked and lived to see his childhood fantasies come to life under the soft glow of "on air" lights for nearly 30 years-- and having the honor of sharing these stories of his broadcasting forefathers and heroes lets that feeling *keep on riding...*

FOR MORE OF
BUFFALO'S
BROADCASTING &
POP CULTURE
HISTORY...
VISIT
BUFFALOSTORIES.COM